Royalty In Motion

Royalty In Motion

Pastor Michelle Lyston

Edited By: Marsha A. McCormack

Printed In Columbia, South Carolina USA

Royalty In Motion

Royalty In Motion

Copyright © 2019 by Pastor Michelle Lyston.

Library of Congress Control Number: 2019942168
ISBN: 978-1-7320762-4-2

All Rights Reserved. No part of this publication may be reproduced, or transmitted in any form or by any means, electronic or mechanical including photocopying, recording, or by any information storage and retrieval system, without prior permission in writing from the copyright owner.

Edited by: Marsha A. McCormack
Cover Design by: Johann D. A. Williams

Scripture quotations are taken from the New King James Version/Thomas Nelson Publishers, Nashville: Thomas Nelson Publishers. Copyright © 1982. Used by permission. All Rights Reserved.

This book was printed in Columbia, South Carolina, United States of America

Dedication

This book is dedicated to:

The King of Kings, the Almighty Father, Elohim, the Most High God, to Whom be all glory, honor, dominion and power forever and ever!

My earthly king, Apostle Dr. Steve Lyston. It is my honor and a blessing to stand beside you and with you to do the will of our King.

My queen-in-the-making *Hannah* and future kings *Joshua* and *Shevado* – you are Royalty. Never forget it.

My sisters *Marsha McCormack*, *Patrice Williams*, *Nicole Bertram* and *Colleen Bruce* – I consider you *Royalty In Motion*

My kingly brothers *Johann Williams*, *Kurt McCormack*, *Andre Cummings*, *Dwayne Cummings*, and *Marlon Cummings* – always be the kings God created you to be.

Bishop Dr. Doris Hutchinson – a true lady and *Royalty in Motion*.

Zelma Thomas – thank you for raising up a king for me.

The memory of my father – *Stannard A. Williams* – who led and covered his family like a true king should.

Royalty In Motion

The memory of my mother – *Hazeth B. Williams* – who exuded grace and taught her daughters, through her example and guidance, how to be the queens God created us to be; and taught her son what to look for in a queen.

Every woman God created, regardless of race, color or creed – with the King of Kings you are *Royalty In Motion.*

Ola "Auntie Ola" Duhaney, for your love and devotion to our family. You are special to me.

Lasmin "Auntie Sweet" Reece, for your genuine love and care for our family through every circumstance. You are truly uncommon – we love you.

Nadra Brotherton, for looking out for "mommy and daddy" over the years. Your love and care for me and my family are absolutely invaluable.

Sophia DiMuccio, for your prayers, genuine love, encouragement, and unselfish support – standing graciously with me and my family in some of the most challenging seasons.

Carolyn Grant, for genuine love, support and dedication over many years. Your unwavering care without hesitation – I cannot forget.

Natalie Green, for your continued kindness, genuine love and support for so many years – you are one of a kind.

Also, to:

Apostle Dr. Juliet Bradford
Jasmine and Stanley Calixte
Janice Dixon

Royalty In Motion

Therese Forbes
Rackel James
Omanso and Petagaye Jolly`
Letisha Livingstone
Dr. Yvonne Munroe-Whitmore
Maureen Phillips
Dr. Simone Van Horn
Andrea L. M. Wilson

Table of Contents

		Page
Foreword		9
Introduction		11
Chapter 1	The Queen Within You	16
Chapter 2	God's Royal Daughters Must Rise Up	32
Chapter 3	Be Royalty In Motion For The King	38
Chapter 4	Fast Like A Queen	50
Chapter 5	Maintaining Your Prayer Life	58
Chapter 6	Know The King's Ordinances	77
Chapter 7	Be Fearless And Faithful	84
Chapter 8	Stay Focused! We Are The Salt Of The Earth	92
Chapter 9	The Attack On The Womb	99
Chapter 10	Be Poised And Positioned For Greater	115

Chapter 11	Personal Protocols	137
Chapter 12	Are You Royalty In Motion?	149
Bibliography		163

Foreword

One of the reasons there are so many problems eating away at the society is that we are arduously seeking to ensure that individuals achieve academic goals and acquire degrees in order to excel in their jobs. But very little emphasis is placed on teaching them how to live. The Family is the training ground for higher and greater authority. It is the foundation for good governance.

The increase in the levels of child abuse globally is a reflection of the general instability of family life and laws to address this matter are irrelevant. It is going to take more than laws to deal with this issue. We need virtuous women to help who recognize their value and royalty to bring balance, which will lead to global change in all sectors.

The Bible says older women should teach the younger women that is part of mentorship. We need Godly mentors regardless of gender. Someone could never work in the king's palace and be effective unless they are taught the right things – how to walk, how to speak, how to attire yourself, protocols especially on when to speak and how to carry yourself in the palace and when dealing with visitors to the palace.

We need a change now and the nation needs the virtuous, royal daughters to rise up, make the difference and set an example for the next generation.

Remember, we are created as royalty, so we have to function as Royalty.

Apostle Dr. Steve Lyston
Restoration World Outreach Ministries Inc.

Introduction

In 2008, my husband and I went through one of the most painful seasons we had ever been through personally up to that point – the loss of a child. Little did I know that the experience would help me to better understand my purpose, who I am as a woman in service of the King of Kings, and why the enemy fights us so fiercely as women – royal daughters of the King - with such intensity and utter vehemence.

Genesis 3: 13 – 16 says, *"And the Lord God said to the woman, "What is this you have done?" The woman said, "The serpent deceived me, and I ate." So the Lord God said to the serpent: "Because you have done this, you are cursed more than all cattle, and more than every beast of the field; on your belly you shall go, and you shall eat dust all the days of your life. And I will put enmity between you and the woman, and between your seed and her Seed; He shall bruise your head, and you shall bruise His heel."*

Not only did the Most High God, Elohim our Creator cause the woman to be the carrier of the Seed that would ultimately defeat him, but the Almighty God – our Father and King, has granted every woman the privilege of the *capacity* to carry the seed. Our very existence as women, reminds the devil that He is already defeated through Jesus Christ – who became the Seed of a woman, as God had declared. Women are the devil's constant reminder that he no longer has the opportunity to go to heaven, but

instead has an eternal sentence in hell – in a lake of fire – his ultimate defeat! Indeed, the warfare is not really about us individually, it's about what we represent: his final defeat and God's eternal victory. Recognize that the same "woman" that the enemy tricked and defeated in the garden, was the same "woman" through whom the devil's ultimate defeat came!

Women, we have the potential to make a mess, but in His Divine Wisdom, our Creator has empowered us with the capacity to fix it. We are catalysts for change with the capacity to bring healing.

Our Heavenly Father, Creator and King, wants us to come to the realization that despite our mistakes, flaws, failures, issues and our fears, within each of us is the capacity to rise above that and accomplish great things for God, through Jesus Christ, by the power of His Holy Spirit. We have the capacity to positively change lives and the direction of nations by simply walking in obedience to God, His Word and His instructions, believing what He says about us, and strengthening our families by teaching our children the Word of God; by walking with our husbands in the will of God; by loving our royal sisters with real, pure love and without prejudice; by standing with our kingly brothers, and be whom God has created us to be.

We have the capacity to be *Royalty In Motion* for the King of Kings - to authoritatively and with Divine grace, bring change to nations, with the gifts and talents He has deposited within us. Don't allow fear and rejection to propel you into a life of fear, doubt and hopelessness, and push us out of the will of God and abort our purpose.

The gift of Salvation through Jesus Christ, affords us the privileged opportunity to do more and be more than we ever thought we could in our lives – with our lives, but it's a choice. That is *your* decision.

1 Samuel 10: 25 "Then Samuel explained to the people the *behavior of royalty*, and wrote it in a book and laid it up before the Lord. And Samuel sent all the people away, every man to his house."

Royalty In Motion

CHAPTER 1

The Queen Within You

From The Beginning

"And the Lord God caused a deep sleep to fall on Adam, and he slept; and He took one of his ribs, and closed up the flesh in its place. Then the rib which the Lord God had taken from man He made into a woman, and He brought her to the man. And Adam said: "This is now bone of my bones and flesh of my flesh; she shall be called <u>Woman</u>, because she was taken out of Man." (Genesis 2: 21 – 23)

Women. From the moment we were created by God – King of the Universe, we were peculiar, uncommon and a full of mystery, with immense potential, beauty and greatness locked within. The Creator and Father of Mankind created us from a rib – the rib of a man – so we cannot ignore nor negate our strong connection with man (the male of the species). The Omnipotent God put the man to sleep, took one rib from him and made that rib into woman! What an amazing God! No wonder men can't figure us out on their own; God had put man to sleep, while He worked on us. What this tells us is that if a man wants to identify his "rib", he must seek the Creator first; and if he truly wants to understand her, he *must* again seek the Creator. Furthermore, as women, we also will need to go to our Heavenly Father so that He can fashion us into the priceless, favor-filled vessel of honor He needs us to be for Him, and the one to which we are to cleave. Ultimately, the creation of mankind automatically requires relationship with the Creator.

The moment the enemy of our souls – the devil – saw the potential in mankind and the relationship that existed between God and man, He absolutely despised mankind and everything about us; and he recognized that the way to destroy mankind is to sever that pure relationship between God and man and inject fear, doubt and guilt into the equation. He knew he couldn't defeat God, but he could attack God's creation – His children and cause them to lose sight of who they really are and what they are capable of in God. He has been doing that since the beginning of time and it continues today.

But all is not lost! There is HOPE! God sent Jesus Christ His Son, as our Redeemer, because of His love for us. Our Redeemer bought us back, so-to-speak, and paid for us by His Sacrifice – the shedding of His Blood on the Cross (the Crucifixion), His Resurrection and His Ascension to the Right Hand of God the Father in Heaven gives us Eternal Hope. Through that act of insurmountable love, Jesus offers to us salvation from eternal death and torment in Hades with Lucifer – the devil and all the forces of evil he works with. Through Jesus Christ we have hope! As we develop our relationship with the Savior –Jesus Christ – then access is granted once again, and we can once again know who we really are in Him, who we are to become, what our purpose is individually and collectively, and ultimately, spend eternity with our Creator, God and King!

Queen Emerging

From the beginning of woman's existence, the enemy has sought to use three (3) main weapons to attack us and influence our actions and decision-making:

1. Doubt

2. The Spirit of Fear

3. The Spirit of Rejection

and as is outlined in Genesis 3, he started the conversation with heresy – he only told Eve half-truths regarding what God said. (That is why it is important for us to know the Word of God ourselves.) Eve embraced the enemy's lies and took them as truth. Recognize, however, that there are three (3) main reasons someone would embrace a lie as the truth:

1. Lack of Knowledge

2. **Unbelief**

3. **Improper/Impure Motives** (State of the Heart)

Nevertheless, thanks be to God Almighty Who not only sent Jesus Christ to redeem us, but after the Ascension of Jesus Christ to Heaven, sent the Holy Spirit the Comforter, to teach, guide, direct and help us in every area of life so that we can become and remain who God needs us to be – individually and collectively – for His purpose and glory.

For many women, if not all, our past haunts us. The enemy brings constant reminders of who we used to be, what we used to do, who we used to hang around with, old bad habits and attitudes. The devil will also try to bring up the circumstances/situations within which we were born. For example, being born out of wedlock, through rape, abuse or incest, being born within a loveless marriage, or a marriage of convenience, and yet there are others who were born to parents who were married to each other, loved each other and had no of the issues mentioned before. My Royal Sisters, whatever the circumstances were surrounding our birth, regardless of the mess we may be, God loves us. He created us with great purpose, and the moment we surrender our hearts to the Lord and accept the Salvation of Jesus Christ, He cleans us up, renews, repairs and restores us and sets us on a new path, so that we can fulfill our purpose and walk in the steps He has ordered for our lives. Abba wants us to be the Royal Daughters He originally created us to be. He wants us to emerge from the mess, the sin, the mediocre, the "less than", the lack of knowledge, the doubt, the fear, the rejection and the commonness, and rise up to emerge as the queens we are through Him. The true queens must emerge and reclaim our royal heritage through the King of Kings.

The King of Kings wants you to know and embrace your royal heritage so that the devil will not triumph over you, but instead, you will rise as royalty.

Ezekiel 16: 3 – 14 reminds us,

"…'Thus says the Lord God to Jerusalem: "Your birth and your nativity are from the land of Canaan; your father was an Amorite and your mother a Hittite. As for your nativity, on the day you were born your navel cord was not cut, nor were you washed in water to cleanse you; you were not rubbed with salt nor wrapped in swaddling cloths. No eye pitied you, to do any of these things for you, to have compassion on you; but you were thrown out into the open field, when you yourself were loathed on the day you were born. "And when I passed by you and saw you struggling in your own blood, I said to you in your blood, 'Live!' Yes, I said to you in your blood, 'Live!' I made you thrive like a plant in the field; and you grew, matured, and became very beautiful. Your breasts were formed, your hair grew, but you were naked and bare. "When I passed by you again and looked upon you, indeed your time was the time of love; so I spread My wing over you and covered your nakedness. Yes, I swore an oath to you and entered into a covenant with you, and you became Mine," says the Lord God. "Then I washed you in water; yes, I thoroughly washed off your blood, and I anointed you with oil. I clothed you in embroidered cloth and gave you sandals of badger skin; I clothed you with fine linen and covered you with silk. I adorned you with ornaments, put bracelets on your wrists, and a chain on your neck. And I put a jewel in your nose, earrings in your ears, and a beautiful crown on your head.

Thus you were adorned with gold and silver, and your clothing was of fine linen, silk, and embroidered cloth. You ate pastry of fine flour, honey, and oil. You were exceedingly beautiful, and succeeded to royalty. Your fame went out among the nations because of your beauty, for it was perfect through My splendor which I had bestowed on you," says the Lord God.

Recognize that your past, where you are from and who you were born to does not determine your future. God has for you a future and a hope, and as He says in Jeremiah 29: 11, He knows the thoughts He thinks toward you. However, you – by your mindset, attitude, level of faith, willingness to be processed/trained, willingness to submit to the will of God and determination to fulfill your purpose will determine whether you walk into that future or not. Embrace the Lord's plan and will for your life and you will begin your journey to becoming not just Royalty by title, but you will actively begin your journey to becoming Royalty In Motion – action, not talk.

The Journey Begins

Your journey to becoming Royalty In Motion begins when you recognize and accept the fact that you are uncommon and should not settle for less than what God has for you. The next step is understanding that you are the Daughter of a King, and as such, you must separate yourself from the things and situations that diminish your value in your own mind. You are priceless to your Creator and your value is far above priceless gems. So that the King of Kings wants you to carry yourself not as an arrogant, overbearing, boisterous woman with a bad attitude and no morals, but as a daughter, humble, patient, submitted to the King, precious in the sight of her Father, who knows her value, is confident and meek (not weak), who is not afraid to be set apart, and who will boldly embrace the will of God for her life.   2 Corinthians 6: 16 – 18 reminds us, *"And what agreement has the temple of God with idols? For you are the temple of the living God. As God has said: "I will dwell in them and walk among them. I will be their God, and they shall be My people." Therefore "Come out from among them and be separate, says the Lord. Do not touch what is unclean, and I will receive you. I will be a Father to you, and you shall be My sons and daughters, says the Lord Almighty."*

Let The Queenly Character Emerge

A queen knows that she represents God, her family, herself, and everyone/every group to which she is connected in any way, and she always strives to do it well.

A queen knows the value of honor and does so in every capacity. But the most important attribute and hallmark of a true queen is that she maintains and values a strong relationship with God her King through Jesus Christ, by the power of the Holy Spirit. She knows that such a relationship opens the door for His Presence on her life, so that her desire and goal is always to honor Him in whatever she does; and that affects family, ministry, social/personal life, business and every other area of her life.

As queen, she has the responsibility of preparing successors, (Proverbs 22: 6) so to a certain level, she has the charge of not only teaching her daughters how to be queens and how to do it well, but also to teach her sons how to be kings, and teach them how to maintain their kingship. That includes each one selecting the right queen to help him maintain his kingship his inheritance and his birthright, and to identify the one who will also teach their sons and daughters to be kings and queens.

A true queen must live and teach moral leadership and model behavior not just to her family, but also to those God allows her to encounter and influence. She cannot live any kind of lifestyle, engage in gossip, function on sheer emotions; she is to be set apart in how she deals

with situations she faces, how she sets examples for others to follow. She sets high standards in how she functions and carries herself and she functions with grace and under grace to do whatever God has called or allowed her to do.

A true queen and royal daughter is loyal to her kings – her earthly king, who is her husband; and her Heavenly King and Father.

A true queen, when she is single, recognizes that she cannot afford to be unequally yoked, and therefore, waits for her Creator and King to send her earthly king and she knows that neither marriage nor ministry are competitions between her king and herself, but instead recognizes that they are gifts from God – opportunities – to allow them to fulfill their God-given purpose. They complement each other as they do so, to the Glory of God.

A true queen understands what submission really is and is not offended by it. She embraces it and recognizes the value of submission and what it represents. She does not fear it - she embraces it.

A true queen who is married to her king must know the significance and importance of spiritual warfare in the effort to protecting her head and the power of intercession, fasting and worship.

The Proverbs 31 Queen

In the first nine (9) verses of Proverbs 31, King Lemuel recounted the things his mother taught him to be the king he was created to be. The remaining 22 verses were about her teaching him how to maintain his kingship and understanding how to identify the wife who was capable of helping him maintain his role and his wealth – his "help meet".

The woman of Proverbs 31 was the mother of a King, which also means she was a queen in her own right. She follows the direction of the Lord God to direct her steps especially concerning her family. This is a significant contrast of the woman who chooses to lean on her own understanding. (*Genesis 3*)

Proverbs 31 reveals to us that a queen does more than sit on a throne. She is not lazy, always expecting to be handed everything she wants, but she is willing to actively participate in life – positioned with her king, empowering her children leading by example while pursuing her Heavenly King. She knows what the throne represents and what is required to maintain the legacy of the kingdom; and she is willing to get involved. She understands that with her royal status comes responsibilities on many levels.

Politically, she functions with a sense of duty and responsibility to her community and nation, and takes that responsibility very seriously. She helps to maintain unity and brings a sense of stability and continuity to her environment.

Executively, she makes decisions in/for her family and subsequently, her community to foster growth, proper development and ultimately success.

Royalty Submits to Leadership

Hebrews 13: 17 reminds us, *"Obey your leaders and submit to them, for they are keeping watch over your souls, as those who will have to give an account. Let them do this with joy and not with groaning, for that would be of no advantage to you."* Furthermore, 1 Peter 2: 18 says, *"Servants, be submissive to your masters with all fear, not only to the good and gentle, but also to the harsh."* In addition to this, 1 Thessalonians 5: 12 – 13 also says, *"And we urge you, brethren, to recognize those who labor among you, and are over you in the Lord and admonish you, 13 and to esteem them very highly in love for their work's sake. Be at peace among yourselves."*

Submission to leaders is very important to the King of Kings, because each leader – whether gentle or harsh, represents Him at some level. Submission to those He allows to be over you also shows that you:

1. Love the Lord your God

2. Respect and honor His wisdom in allowing them to be your leaders

3. Trust Him to help you grow under the leaders He set over you

4. Are willing to humbly submit to His authority by submitting to those He allows over you

5. Want the will of God for your life,

6. Willingly embrace the process God is allowing you to go though and;

7. Are interested in your own spiritual growth and development.

Submitting to leadership has more benefit for you than for the leader. Everything you do in submission to your leaders reflects on you and everything and everyone to whom you are connected – including the King you serve.

That being said, it therefore means that submission to leadership is also a weapon against the enemy (since the devil loves it when we walk in disobedience), and submission is also our biggest method of protection, since the devil can't legally attack when we are walking in obedience to God.

Royalty Submits To The King

Submission is key to our success at any and every level in every area of our lives. In school we have to submit our work. Whether we think it is good or not we still must submit it to someone who has the authority to scrutinize it, even if we think we know more than the one who is scrutinizing it. Recognize that submission is not about who knows more than whom. It is about who has the authority to help usher you into your destiny and on the path to fulfilling your purpose.

Many people today often make the mistake of thinking that they submit to someone only if they believe that person is more knowledgeable than they are, or more academically qualified, more connected, more everything, than they are on a physical level, or if they are more financially stable or "secure". They have no problem submitting to that person and have no problem following the instructions such a person gives. As a result, many make their decision to submit based on what they see externally and have become comfortable believing that the best way to determine if someone is worth submitting to, worth listening to, worth networking/connecting with, worth being the protégé of, worth taking to lunch, worth being seen with, worth investing in, worth loving, worth getting to know! Yet in all of this, some of them say they want to be like Jesus. (*2 Kings 5, Matthew 3 esp. verse 13; 1 Samuel 16: 7; Jeremiah 17: 7 – 10*)

This kind of thought process, this way of thinking is what hinders many, robs them of the blessings of God for their lives, and stops them from fulfilling their purpose and the call of God on their lives. This kind of mindset causes them to make decisions for their lives that bring them down the wrong path – steers them in the wrong direction, opens the door for pride to become a stronghold in their lives, and prevents their spiritual growth and processing for God's glory.

Recognize that this is not something that takes place in the church, or in "church/ministry" circles – this happens in every facet, in every area at every level of our society! But if we want true prosperity in our lives, prosperity that is not all about Money. Instead, it is about true and comprehensive success in the family – mentally, spiritually, financially and emotionally. It is about the flourishing of our physical health *and* our souls. So, we must follow the divine principles of God concerning Submission. We must submit – not to whom feel – but to whom God says.

Generally, we as human beings often think we know it all or that we are experts, especially when we have seen or done something before or if we have had a similar experience before. We must, however, recognize that our experiences give us exposure to situations to allow us a certain level of understanding – it doesn't cause us to know it all. We can never be able to know the full story on a person or a situation by looking at the external picture – the physical features and attire, or the academic achievements, how good someone looks in their social media pictures, how eloquently they speak or not, how logical their conversations/reasoning sounds, how modern their cars are, the styles or locations of their homes – these do not give you the full picture of who they are or of their character, level of integrity, skills/talents, anointing and spiritual authority.

D-avid as king still had to submit to the prophetic voice of God through His prophets (*2 Samuel 7*)

According to 2 Kings 5, Naaman was the captain of the host, the army of the king of Syria. Naaman was in a very powerful position as the king's go-to guy for all things war-related. He was very highly regarded by the king as a solider. Yet he had to submit to the recommendations of a lowly servant girl who worked for him – in his house, to go see the prophet of God, Elisha in order to receive healing. His king allowed him to go, sending him with a letter to the King of Israel explaining the situation, and he, then had to submit to the instructions of God through His servant the prophet Elisha.

Matthew 3: 13 – 17 reveals the true submission of Jesus Christ which is an example for us all to follow. Many times, as Christians we are tested regarding our faith; our level of trusting God/trust in God; our patience, our love for God; our love for our neighbor and so on.

When Jesus came willingly to this earth to die for us all, He died for those who were before He came, for those at the time He was on earth and for those who were not born yet and that includes you and me. He knew the magnitude of His mission, yet He submitted to execute the mission.

Our Master Submitted, So Should We

John 13: 15 – 17 says, *"For I have given you an example, that you should do as I have done to you. Most assuredly, I say to you, a servant is not greater than his master; nor is he who is sent greater than he who sent him. If you know these things, blessed are you if you do them."*

Our Master, Jesus Christ by His example laid out in the Scriptures, lived a life of submission to His Father and to the instructions of His Father. (*John 17: 1 – 5*)

Matthew 3: 13 – 17 says, *"Then Jesus came from Galilee to John at the Jordan to be baptized by him. And John tried to prevent Him, saying, "I need to be baptized by You, and are You coming to me?" But Jesus answered and said to him, "Permit it to be so now, for thus it is fitting for us to fulfill all righteousness." Then he allowed Him. When He had been baptized, Jesus came up immediately from the water; and behold, the heavens were opened to Him, and He saw the Spirit of God descending like a dove and alighting upon Him. And suddenly a voice came from heaven, saying, "This is My beloved Son, in whom I am well pleased."*

Submission is one of the key principles that is exercised in both heaven and earth. Lucifer was evicted from Heaven, because he allowed pride to consume him and as a result, he rebelled and refused to submit. (*Isaiah 14: 12 – 21*) Jesus knew the importance of submitting to the authorities around Him. He also knew that while He created the heavens and the earth, He also established **order** in the earth to govern the earth and everything and everyone within. If Jesus went against His own principle, then it would mean that the enemy would have had legal right to attack Him and destroy the earth.

1. Jesus submitted to the instructions of His Heavenly Father.

2. Jesus submitted to becoming human for our sake – to become the spiritually legal sacrifice for us as human beings. So, He submitted to what was below His level in every way.

3. Jesus submitted to the earthly authority of John the Baptist and was baptized by Him.

4. Jesus submitted to Baptism – one of the principles we as human beings must engage in as an outward declaration that we are no longer of the world, and have completely accepted everything that is of God, His Will, His calling on our life, His Word, His instructions, His way of doing things, His principles – everything God says we are to have and be. For Jesus, Baptism was His official earthly acceptance of the mission He was on; so it was not only Him leaving Heaven to do the task, but accepting it officially here on earth. He was totally submitted to the God the Father and King.

Recognize that submission not only maintains order, but is the foundation for humility and keeps pride at bay. One person's pride can destroy nations. Submission also covers us from the attacks of the enemy. When we are submitted, we are obeying God's Word and are in the will of God. In doing so, the enemy cannot legally attack us.

CHAPTER 2

God's Royal Daughters Must Rise Up

"But when the fullness of the time had come, God sent forth His Son, born of a woman, born under the law, to redeem those who were under the law, that we might receive the adoption as sons." And because you are sons, God has sent forth the Spirit of His Son into your hearts, crying out, "Abba, Father!" (Galatians 4: 4 – 6)

Interestingly this Scripture makes reference to "sons" of God the King, yet it includes both males and females, and it says to us as women that we have that privilege, authority, and opportunity to call upon Him as Father at all times. It is also a reminder that we daughters have lost sight of our roles and goals, not only within the family, and community He allows us to be a part of, but also in the Body of Christ and the society in general. This is in part due to the breakdown that we, His daughters, have allowed to take place in our houses, in His house, and in the nation.

Hold The Reigns Again

As women, we are the main gatekeepers especially in the family. Gatekeepers are key in all areas of our society. Gatekeepers must be discerners and be willing to learn because they determine who goes in and who stays out. The enemy, in order to get to the head – Adam, the enemy went after the gatekeeper – Eve, and when the enemy gets by the gatekeeper, the head becomes an easy target, and that is so in all areas – family, community, businesses, governments and nations.

As gatekeepers, our assignment is given by the King and once the King has spoken, regardless of whatever else is said by any other voice, Gatekeepers must follow the instructions issued by the King.

As Gatekeepers:

1. We have stopped interceding so pride has entered the Church and our personal lives. We stopped interceding so the spiritual defense we had against dishonesty, lack, corruption, lust, betrayal, disorder and immorality. The Lord wants us as women to revisit Proverbs 31 because while we have read that Scripture and we highlight it every

Mothers' Day, we have missed the most important verse of that Scripture which is verse 1 which says "*The words of King Lemuel, the utterance <u>which his mother taught him</u>*"

2. We are not spending time in the Presence of the Lord as we should, so we are not recognizing what is really taking place in our society: The spiritual warfare has intensified to the point where the enemy is convincing men that they are women, and women that they are men, and that when God created them He made a mistake. The real goal of the enemy is to shift men and women out of position, out of God's Divine Order, and rob them of their authority. Regardless of our opinions about the issue, the Word of God tells us in Genesis that:

    a) men were created by God to be the head and covering for their families, and

    b) women were made the carriers of the seed, and the arrows would defeat the devil and destroy his plans.

We as women have the wombs to carry the potential to defeat the enemy and gain victories in our lives, our Church and our nation. This is why there is such a warfare to get the nation to embrace abortion, and for gender change to be accepted. This is why there is such a battle with pregnancies and why miscarriages are so prevalent – especially in this era. Our wombs represent God's Original and Divine Plan for mankind's continuity.

3. We stopped teaching our sons and daughters how to function with integrity in their lives, so:

    a) We do not teach them not to rob God of the Tithe or give unto the Lord anymore;

    b) We do not give our children perimeters and limits anymore;

    c) we let them watch anything at any time because it takes too much out of us to marshal them and train them in the way they should go according to the Word of God. Meanwhile, the world is teaching them through the cartoons and television programs how to do witchcraft, how to be disrespectful and dishonorable to parents when the Word of God tells us to honor our father and mother.

    d) We do not teach them how to be sensitive to the needs of others around us and how to care; we are not teaching them how to treat the elders in our society with honor and respect.

4. The older women stopped teaching the younger women God's Word in Titus 2: 1 – 5 *"But as for you, speak the things which are proper for sound doctrine: that the older men be sober, reverent, temperate, sound in faith, in love, in patience; the older women likewise, that they be reverent in behavior, not slanderers, not given to much wine, teachers of good things—that they admonish the young women to love their husbands, to love their children, to be*

discreet, chaste, homemakers, good, obedient to their own husbands, that the word of God may not be blasphemed."

5. Our women have now become so focused on their own physical appearance and sexuality and on how to use those physical things to get or access what they need or want or want to get done. Instead of using the God-given weapon of prayer, and instead of seeking God for the solutions He wants to give us to the problems we are facing – whether personally or nationally; and instead of staying in the presence of God to access and maintain the blessings and victories He wants to give us in order to build the Kingdom of God, our women are more focused on hair and make-up, learning how to lap dance to keep a man – or "add spice" to their marriage relationship, or to compare themselves with other women. As a result, the Hair, Makeup and Clothing Industries are being built up and the building of God's Kingdom and the strengthening of the nation in God is being put to the back burner, hence the consequences we are all experiencing.

We as God's Royal Daughters must pick up our role again as Gatekeepers in the family and in the Kingdom and emerge as the queens He created us to be.

God is calling out women:

1. Who are not easily fazed by or fearful of negative words;

2. Who are not focused on what people have to say about them and those who do not use public opinion to determine who they are and how they should function.

3. Who are determined to see order restored to the Family, the Body of Christ, to their communities, to the society and to their nation.

4. Who understand that men are not their competition but their partners in building up and empowering their children for a better future.

5. Who are not afraid to boldly live by the principles, instructions, precepts and Word of God, and mentor others to do the same.

God is searching for those women, those Royal Daughters who know that they are royalty but still function in genuine humility. Such ones know that according to God's Word in Psalm 139: 14 they are fearfully and wonderfully made and they each have a purpose to fulfill.

The Heavenly Father is searching for daughters who know how and are willing to fight fearlessly and fiercely all the negative declarations that have been spewed over the nation, over the Church, over the institutions of Family and Marriage and over our sons and daughters, that cancel the negative by speaking the positive word – the Word of God and declare it.

CHAPTER 3

Be Royalty In Motion For The King

Women are coming to the fore now more than ever before and many are entering positions of great influence and high-level leadership. Even in Eastern nations where women did not have a say or a vote or no rights whatsoever, their voices are getting louder and louder and can no longer be ignored.

This is a critical time for nations and particularly for women throughout the globe, because the tide has shifted, and women are rising to be decision-makers in more than just household issues. Today, communities, organizations and nations are being run and steered by women, not behind the scene, but from the top of the ladder of success.

Yet, with everything we see happening around the world today – the fight for abortion rights, the gender issues of the day, the fight for the rights of the child, human trafficking, corruption at all levels, increase in the billion-dollar sex trade, it is so easy to feel helpless and hopeless against such a formidable set of opponents to our true purpose. It is time for us to be Royalty, in motion for the King of Kings.

Being Royalty In Motion

We were not created to simply exist! We have not been placed on the earth at this specific time as an afterthought or on a whim! We are purposed with greatness, and the King of Kings has decreed it to be so. Being *Royalty In Motion* for the King simply means that we, as His Royal Daughters must be in active service for Him. We must engage in action for our King, to bring positive change to families, communities, and ultimately our nation.

There has to be that sense of urgency within us to do all we can to be catalysts for effective and positive change everywhere we are, and resist the oppression, injustices and the inequalities we are seeing and experiencing; especially those things that go against the God's Principles and His Word.

No Gender Competition

Both genders, male and female, have been created with specific roles and purposes and we need to know what those are so that we can fulfill our purpose and potential and walk in the greatness for which we are made. Hosea 4: 6 says *"My people are destroyed for lack of knowledge..."* We need to get into, embrace and stay in the Presence and the Word of God. That's how we will know our purpose and understand our roles. The Creator knows the secrets and mysteries of His creation.

Royalty, let us NOT get caught up in gender competitions, racial segregation, classist behavior, and sister-sabotage, and become filled with pride and hatred. Let us NOT be instigators nor facilitators of division, brokenness and hate crimes, we have the capacity to change all that through Jesus Christ by the power of His Holy Spirit. Our worship can break chains, bring down walls and change the atmosphere. Let's do that and do it well – in Spirit and in Truth. We are game-changers – so change the game in our favor! But know that you can only do that when you stay in God's Presence! Start or strengthen your relationship with Him.

You have within you the capacity to accomplish greatness and bring solutions to the table – any table. God has equipped you with the capacity, grace, favor, strength and the opportunity of His Presence that you may initialize, influence and affect environments, situations, processes, systems, communities and the course of governments and nations. But know also that it must all be according to the Will of God. So, as His Royal Daughter, you are required to know His will for you and His purpose for your life, and how to proceed from your present position – for your good and for His glory!

Every situation you have faced has been your training process! Every struggle/problem you have faced that the enemy would use to push you down was an opportunity for you to learn to soar – because you are an overcomer, more than a conqueror through Jesus Christ – you are an eagle! Remember always that "*all things work together for good to those who love God, to those who are the called according to His purpose."* (Romans 8: 28)

Royal Daughter of the Most High God, we are called:

1. To bring forth the seed that shall bruise the head of the enemy with the heel. *(Genesis 3: 15)*

2. To raise and teach your sons to be the kings they are created to be. *(Proverbs 31: 1 - 9)*

3. To raise and teach your daughters how to become the queens they are created to be. *(Ruth 3)*

4. To be the example of virtue, grace, love, wisdom, entrepreneurship, elegance, class, strength that those around us need to see and be to inspire the manifestation of greatness. *(Proverbs 31)*

5. To rise out of our comfort zone and fulfill our purpose through the God's Divine wisdom and strategy. *(Esther 4)*

6. To know and embrace the fact that we cannot accomplish God's will for our lives nor can we truly know and understand our purpose without being in His Presence and maintaining it on our lives. *(Psalm 91: 1, Jeremiah 29: 11)*

7. Our King is counting on us to represent Him well. We cannot afford to be Vashti. *(Esther 1)*

Royalty In Motion

It is time for us to rise as Esthers in this season, in this time and allow God to position us for the sake of the Kingdom, for the sake of souls, for the sake of our children, for the sake of our nation, for the fulfillment of our purpose and for HIS GLORY!!!!

The King of kings is calling us out of our comfort zone and into His Presence – to rise up and be the Esthers of our time. We have to wake up, be less absorbed with ourselves and choose to be Royalty, in motion/action for Him!

We need to love and honor your kingly brothers; love and respect your royal sisters and recognize that color, culture, race, status – none of it matters. What matters is honoring our Father – the King – in EVERYTHING we do.

Do you know the potential within you? Do you know that like Esther (Esther 2), you are a queen? You are Royalty! That is why you must trust God to take you through the process so you can become what He ordained – become Royalty, In Motion, for Him. The process is a good thing.

Embracing Esther

While Vashti and Esther were both queens, one's actions represented the kingdom of darkness and the other represented the Kingdom of God. It is very important to distinguish the Vashtis from the Esthers.

Vashti was a type of Jezebel – she functioned in rebellion and one act of rebellion can topple an entire kingdom. Jezebel, although a queen, was the daughter of a high priest of Baal. She was herself a high priestess of Baal. Vashti was rebellious, disrespectful, dishonorable in her actions and had the wrong attitude toward leadership, toward her head and toward the king – she refused to submit to the king's instructions. She was much like Jezebel was in her day, who rebelled against the great prophets of the day and defied every God-given instruction through them. She did not listen to the king; instead she ruled the king. She had a domineering character and dictated to her head – her husband and king; and oppressed and killed those around her who disagreed with her or did not do exactly as she said. Vashti received an instruction from her king and publicly refuted and rejected it.

Unfortunately, there are many women today, who have the same traits, and function with many of the same qualities, and it is those attitudes, behavior and mindset that hinder many women from walking into the level victory, wisdom, prosperity, blessing and fulfillment of purpose. It does not have to remain that way, but it is a choice.

The first 8 verses of Esther 1 are significant, because it sets the foundation for the level of risk and potential victory for the individuals and nations involved. They outline the measure and magnitude of the kingdom over which King Ahasuerus ruled, and showed the level of influence he had, the wealth he had and to a lesser extent it revealed the kind of order and strength of counsel that surrounded him as king. King Ahasuerus ruled over 127 provinces spanning at least 2 continents Asia and Africa – from India to Ethiopia. (Esther 1: 1)

The Lord could have allowed the story of Esther to begin at Esther 2, but just as He did with the truth of Creation, He allowed the foundation to be visibly laid so that the ultimate victory at the end of the story would be understood and appreciated. God could have simply created you in an adult state and planted you on the planet, but He gave you a backstory and a foundation called childhood and a journey called growing, so that we can appreciate the place to which He is taking us. He wants us to appreciate the destination and the outcome as He causes us to fulfill our purpose. Sometimes we have to revisit the beginning of the story and remember where we are coming from in order to appreciate the journey and the outcome God allows.

So, in Esther 1: 1 – 8, it is clear that King Ahasuerus was a ruler of great power, wealth and influence. As his wife, Queen Vashti also had great influence among the wives of the kings and noblemen her husband ruled over as well as the local women. All eyes were on this power couple.

King Ahasuerus *"...commanded Mehuman, Biztha, Harbona, Bigtha, Abagtha, Zethar, and Carcas, seven eunuchs who served in the presence of King Ahasuerus, to bring Queen Vashti before the king, wearing her royal crown, in order to show her beauty to the people and the officials, for she was beautiful to behold. But Queen Vashti refused to come at the king's command brought by his eunuchs..."* (Esther 1: 10 – 12)

The king called for his wife not simply because he wanted to show her beauty. His goal was not to parade her like property. He called for her to show the stability of their union and by extension, the kingdom, so that their confidence in his capacity to lead the provinces well and maintain peace would be clear to them and also to strengthen their trust in him, thus – again – maintaining peace and unity within the provinces and lead them into prosperity; something that every nation within a commonwealth needs.

Furthermore, regardless of how much a man has, or has the capacity to do, having a sensitive, wise and strong wife by his side – a Proverbs 31 woman – means he can trust her safely and she becomes one of the greatest "assets" to him and to their household. Proverbs 31: 10 – 12 says, *"Who can find a virtuous wife? For her worth is far above rubies. <u>The heart of her husband safely trusts her</u>; so he will have no lack of gain. She does him good and not evil all the days of her life."* Furthermore, Proverbs 19: 14 says, *"Houses and riches are an inheritance from fathers, but a prudent wife is from the Lord."*

Recognize that when God allows you to walk as wife to one of His kings, your queenly responsibilities increase and broaden immediately and exponentially.

Royal Daughter, know that you are a blessing and a giftbox of favor being prepared by God for one of His kings (according to Proverbs 18: 22), not just for you both to enjoy, but to accomplish a greater goal and fulfill your purpose together to the Glory of God! When God brings you as his Royal Daughter together with the king He has ordained for you, you become an uncommon and powerful team in the hands of God, with the potential to execute great things for Him – and that makes the devil afraid.

Refuse To Be Delilah

Delilah was a seductress and her loyalty was to the enemy of God's people and she was driven by the love of money. She seduced and enticed the people of God to divulge information – secrets that can bring the weakening, demise or destruction of God's people. This is another manifestation of the spirit of Jezebel. Delilah preys on the weaknesses and carnality of others and if she is let in, she bonds with people on the carnal level – particularly those who are not discerning – to defeat them through seduction.

Many women today allow themselves to become as Delilah was then, getting close to people and beguiling them to release their secrets and weaknesses to her, and she in turn releases the information to the highest bidder or to those who satisfy her needs/requests more readily.

Recognize that despite the fact that it was Samson she seduced and eventually caused to be captured by the enemy and defeated, the real fight behind it all was the enemy's attempt to attack a very solemn vow and covenant between God and man, and to destroy a people – a nation through the weakness of one man. If Samson had not cried out in repentance to the Lord, then his strength would not have been Spiritually restored making him able to defeat his enemies – the enemies of his people.

God is calling us to holiness and away from carnality, so that we can defeat our enemy. He wants to empower us but we must maintain it with holiness. The moment Samson went in to the harlot, he yielded to his carnal desires, totally disregarded and even dishonored his sacred vows to God. He lowered his standards and dragged his royal status through the mud and opened the door for the enemy to have a field day in his weakest areas.

Take note: The enemy cannot defeat us until we lower our standards (those standards laid out in the word of God, so he can weaken us, and it is at that point that he can infiltrate, divide and destroy. We must maintain the standards of holiness and righteousness.

God wants us, as women, to have a stronger relationship with Him. He wants us to function in integrity and righteousness and align our spirits with His Holy Spirit so that when He moves, speaks, instructs, we will know His voice and move accordingly, under His Divine protection and covering. He wants us to function in His will so that we will not be deceived by the enemy of souls, and so that the enemy will not use us to deceive others.

What Differentiates Ruth From Orpah

Ruth 1: 1 – 5 tells us of Elimelech who, during the time of famine, took his family – his wife Naomi and their two sons Mahlon and Chilion – out of Bethlehem and into a foreign land called Moab for what he may have felt was a better life. Their sons married Moabite women, Orpah and Ruth. But Elimelech, Mahlon and Chilion all died in the land of Moab and the women were left without husbands – and experienced a time of sorrow and suffering. Then Naomi decided to return to her homeland, Bethlehem, because she had heard that the Lord was blessing His people there. She called her daughters-in-law to let them \

know of her decision and told both Orpah and Ruth to go back to their families among their own people. God was giving them the opportunity to choose whether they would go back to their old lifestyle and the gods they served – their comfort zone; or to embrace the ways, lifestyle and the God they had encountered having lived with Naomi. Ultimately, Orpah choose to leave while Ruth chose to cleave to Naomi and serve the True and Living God.

Know Who You Are

Every woman needs to know that she is more than just a face and a body. Furthermore, we cannot afford to be Vashtis, Delilahs and Jezebels when our Father made us *His* Royal Daughters.

We were not created to destroy other people's families/unions and separate fathers from their children. It is not the will nor instruction of God for us to keep men away from their children, divide a union joined in Holy Matrimony, and redirect money meant to support a family unit to yourself. God has special plan for each and all of us, but we must accept and embrace it all.

At the foundation level we are daughters, sisters, wives and mothers. Beyond that, we have occupations, group connections and social situations of which we are a part, and in some cases have responsibilities within them. But, despite all the hats women wear, our varying roles in the family unit carries the greatest weight, because we play an integral role in the spiritual, emotional and social growth and development of our families, and further to that, we have been given the awesome and privileged responsibility to nurture and influence the lives of our children, stand with, support and strengthen our husbands, sisters and brothers, and honor our mothers and fathers – all while representing the King of kings, yielding to Him to mature us into the overcomers, excellent strategists and great influencers and role models He created us to be. We must place greater value on ourselves, see ourselves as He sees us, and strive to be the queens and Royal Daughters we are in Him.

CHAPTER 4

Fast Like A Queen

The importance of Fasting and Prayer in the life of every person cannot be overstated. These are vital and staying in the Presence of God cannot be underestimated or taken for granted.

Know that it there are some things that cannot be dealt with by any other means but through fasting. Matthew 17: 19 – 21 tells us, *"Then the disciples came to Jesus privately and said, "Why could we not cast it out?" So Jesus said to them, "Because of your unbelief; for assuredly, I say to you, if you have faith as a mustard seed, you will say to this mountain, 'Move from here to there,' and it will move; and nothing will be impossible for you. However, this kind does not go out except by prayer and fasting."*

The Esther Fast (The Basics)

This fast is one that must be entered for a specific purpose. It must not be done casually.

This Fast is based on the Scripture in Esther 4: 16 which says, *"Go, gather all the Jews who are present in Shushan, and fast for me; neither eat nor drink for three (3) days, night or day. My maids and I will fast likewise. And so I will go to the king, which is against the law; and if I perish, I perish".*

It is interesting to note that it was not legal for one to go to the king without being called or summoned. In the same way that we cannot just enter into the presence of the Lord in any state, for the glory of the Lord could kill you! A king is revered and must be treated with respect. From the greatest to the least could not go in to him without being called. If they did, the decree was that all should be killed, unless the king held out his scepter to the person, then and only then would their life be spared.

At the time Esther went on the fast, the enemy was seeking to get rid of the entire Jewish nation and was sending out decrees against the Jews to have them killed. But the enemy, Haman, did not realize that his Queen was a Jew.

We must remember that although we are going in to make our requests and petitions known to the King, we must also bring the people of God, the Body of Christ before Him.

What The Esther Fast Entails

It is a simple Fast. Do not drink or eat for three (3) days. During those three (3) days your focus must not be on the food you are not eating, but instead maintain the Presence of God with you wherever you go. Stay focused on putting the issue(s) before the Lord, asking Him also for strategies, direction, grace and wisdom.

The Purpose of This Fast

This fast is an indication to the Lord God that although you know the proper way to enter into the presence of the King; the matter at hand requires His urgent attention.

This fast is for:

1. Direction and strategies for the issue you're facing.

2. Receiving uncommon favor from the king – which in our case is to receive uncommon favor from Almighty God our King.

3. Breakthrough, vindication and intervention from our King.

4. Boldness to do what you have been given the mandate to do

5. Another level of crucifying self and selfish desires and to cause the will of God to become your will

6. Greater wisdom as to how to deal with the enemy in the midst of a serious and deadly situation

What To Do During The Fast

Before the Fast begins, ensure that where you have a health issue, especially where you are taking prescribed medication, you are cleared by your doctor.

On days 1 and 2

Pray as much as possible, try not to get into unnecessary conversations and idle jesting. Even if you work, try to be less vocal about un-edifying or irrelevant issues and most importantly – KEEP PRAYING!

- ✓ Pray for the situations and issues that you are bringing before the Lord.
- ✓ Pray for your brothers and sisters in Christ.
- ✓ Pray for breakthrough for the people of God.
- ✓ Pray for boldness on your part.
- ✓ Pray for uncommon favor.
- ✓ Pray for the anointing.
- ✓ Pray for the glory of God to be made manifest among His people and in you.
- ✓ Pray for the peace of Israel and of Jerusalem.

On the second day, make a list of the requests that you need God's urgent attention on – in other words, document your requests.

On day 3:

1. Put on your royal robes – that is – put on the best set of clothes you have, your makeup and perfume and scented lotions and all that. For men, put on your best suit, your cologne, after shave – your best everything! For Pastors, and other church leaders, put on your best robe.

2. Take the requests you have written down and go before the king, and make those requests known to Him. (It is not that God does not know your needs and requests, but He requires you to abide by the principle of decreeing and establishing. Job 22: 28 started by Him in Genesis 1:3

3. Go before the Lord – whether lying prostrate before Him, kneeling before Him, sitting in His presence – but just go before Him with expectation and in great faith that you will find favor in Him, that He may extend His scepter of favor to you and grant you that which you have brought before Him to be made known to Him.

4. At the time that the Lord urges you to do so, read all the requests you have written aloud and make them known to Him.

5. Let this scripture be a part of your prayer after you have spoken your requests. From Esther 5:8

   "If I have found favor in the sight of the king, and if it pleases the king to grant my petition and fulfill my request, then let your presence dwell with and show yourself strong against my enemies, for those

who are against me are also against You. Grant my petitions and let Your uncommon favor and blessing be upon me."

The Lord will move on your behalf, just Him and do not be anxious – watch Him work for you. He will intervene and the Haman in your life will be hung in your place. The victory will be yours. The enemy is counting on you to be worried and to be overwhelmed by your abstinence from food. But just remember that it is worth it to give up food for three (3) days in order see the will of God for your life be accomplished for and through you. Besides, we've been eating everyday all our lives anyway, what is three (3) days?

Remember, God is working His purpose out in you. Give Him something to work with. Give Him your faith through this Fast and watch Him move nations for you!

Your 'Haman' is any obstacle that has been set up to hurt, harm or destroy you. God will deal with your situation – your 'Haman' – as He sees fit.

As we draw closer and closer to the coming of the Lord, there are a few things we need to remember.

- ✓ The importance of knowing God's Word *(Psalm 119: 11; Isaiah 55: 10 – 11; John 1: 1)*

- ✓ The importance and power of Prayer *(Matthew 6: 5 – 14; Matthew 17: 19 – 21; Matthew 26: 41; Ephesians 6: 12 – 19; James 5: 16; Jude 1)*

- ✓ The necessity and importance of Holiness and Consecration (*1 Peter 1: 13 – 16*)

- ✓ The need for Repentance (*2 Chronicles 7: 14; Joel 2: 12 – 13; 2 Peter 3: 9; Revelation 2: 5*)

- ✓ The value of Fasting (*Esther 4, Daniel 6: 17 – 23; Isaiah 58; Joel 2; Matthew 17: 21*)

- ✓ The power of True Worship (*2 Kings 23: 1 – 25; John 4: 23 – 24*)

- ✓ The need for us to have Pure Hearts (*Psalm 24: 3 – 6; Psalm 51; Matthew 5: 8; 1 Timothy 1: 5*)

- ✓ God's command to go for Souls (*Matthew 28: 18 – 20*)

The way things are today with the major hype in the Body of Christ, particularly among those who are supposed to be prophets of God; their constant campaign to display *their* accuracy in the prophetic gift; the constant competition to see who can fast track their way to Apostleship or who can host the most or the largest meetings, or who has the most elaborate structure with the most up-to-date amenities and technology. This is a blatant misrepresentation of the kingdom of God, our roles as servants of God, the Apostolic and Prophetic offices and of God Himself, and He is not pleased about this at all.

We need to get back to basics and to the true foundation and reason for our Christian faith and walk, and get back to knowing and fulfilling our purpose while pressing toward the goal for the prize of the upward call of God in Christ Jesus. (Philippians 3: 12 – 14)

We need to stop looking at the people who have not yet given their lives and souls to the Lord as less than us. Who are Christians and recognize that they are souls and that they are precious to God. A soul is priceless and we need to go back to God individually and collectively as the Body of Christ and repent for the state of our hearts, and ask Him to give us a genuine and deep love for souls – for the people He created – a love for each other, being of the same Creator and Father.

In Acts 11:1 – 18, the Jews in Judea – apostles and other believers – had heard that the Gentiles had also received the Word of God – they heard that they were preached to and they accepted the Word of God. This bothered them and when the Apostle Peter had come to Jerusalem (in Judea) they argued with him about it.

Understand that the Jews, since the time of Moses, were Divinely instructed to circumcise their boys. This set them apart – it consecrated them. So Gentiles were seen as the uncircumcised and therefore unclean. And they were taught that God did not want them to engage in or partake of anything unclean. So for the Jews, Apostle Peter was rebellious and unclean.

Recognize that if we are to walk and live as true Christians – true disciples and followers of Christ Jesus, then we must first ensure that our hearts are right, not according to how we feel, but right in the sight of God.

CHAPTER 5

Maintaining Your Prayer Life

What is Prayer?

According to The Prophet's Dictionary, *Prayer* is defined as *"Worshipful supplication made to petition a god or higher force; entreating a deity."*

As Christians, Prayer as our direct line to the Lord, the process of communicating with the Almighty God, our Father. Prayer is the means of communication that allows two or more people to interact with the One to Whom they pray; where they can discuss, and respond to each other. God wants us to communicate with Him, in the same way we would on a person-to-person phone call.

Prayer is a commandment of God; God has commanded us to pray to Him, and to Him alone.

1. In times of distress, we must turn to God for help;

2. In times of comfort, we must express our gratitude to God; and

3. When all goes well with us, we must still pray to God daily that He continues to show us His mercy and grant us our daily needs.

These days, sad to say, we have more conversations on our cell phones, tablets, Alexa, Siri and all the other devices that have become a necessity to so many people in our society. It is so very sad that today, we have Bluetooth devices, talking computers and even watches that we speak to more than we speak to God! There are questions concerning the things of Life that we ask of Google, rather than asking them of God!

But we must remember that Prayer is not only a commandment of God, and also the most effective and powerful means of communicating with God. When we pray we approach God in many different ways, but it must always be with respect and honor. In our prayers to God we often address Him as our Merciful Father, or as our Father in Heaven, for God regards us, and we regard ourselves, as His children.

In our earthly familial relationships, it is a part of our human characteristic to speak to or share with those we love, like our family members – a mother, a father, a brother or sister, our children, and more importantly, with Him. God created each of us with the capacity and desire to communicate and share – first with Him our Creator and then with others. We must recognize also, that having been made in His image, He too desires to communicate and share with us His children. We must not deny our Father, the opportunity to share with His children – we are robbing Him and ourselves when we do so. Prayer is one of the main ways we communicate with God.

There are basically **seven (7)** types of Prayer to be found in the Word of God.

1. Prayer of Praise
2. Prayer of Thanksgiving
3. Prayer of Intercession
4. Prayer of Petition & Counter-petition
5. Prayer of Supplication
6. Spiritual Warfare Prayer
7. Corporate Prayer (Prayer of Agreement)

Prayer of Praise (Acts 16: 26)

A Prayer of Praise is all about God. We ask for nothing, we seek nothing for ourselves, we focus on nothing else but God Himself. The Lord God admonishes us many times throughout the Bible to ensure that we put Him first (Matthew 6: 33).

1. The Prayer of Praise brings change, transformation, breaks you out of bondage, brings healing and deliverance. Psalm 149: 6 – 9 remind us *"Let the high praises of God be in their mouth, and a two-edged sword in their hand, to execute vengeance on the nations, and punishments on the peoples; to bind their kings with chains, and their nobles with fetters of iron; to execute on them the written judgment—this honor have all His saints. Praise the Lord!"*

2. The Prayer of Praise allows God to minister to our hearts as we earnestly come before Him, so that while we engaged in the Prayer of Praise, He breaks discouragement from us He grants us the garment of praise for the spirit of heaviness (Isaiah 61: 3), so that we can continue to commune with Him.

Prayer of Thanksgiving

Prayers of Thanksgiving are proclaimed throughout the Bible. In 1 Chronicles 16:7-36, we are shown through David's song an excellent example of **four (4)** elements included in true thanksgiving:

1. Remembering what God has done for us.

2. Telling others about it.

3. Showing God's glory to others.

4. Offering gifts of ourselves, our time, and our resources.

We are simply showing our appreciation to the Lord our God – just saying thanks to God in appreciation.

1 Thessalonians 5: 18 reminds us, *"In everything give thanks: for this is the will of God in Christ Jesus concerning you."* Furthermore, the writer of Psalm 75: 1 says, *"To You, O God, do we give thanks, to You do we give thanks; for that Your name is near Your wondrous works declare."*

God has many names and each of His names describe/attest to His character. When we give thanks to the Lord, it is as a result of something He has done to grant us victory in an area of our lives, and He reveals His character to us in our victory.

The Psalms are filled with Songs of Adoration and Thanksgiving to God. Of the 150 psalms, David wrote 73 of them. David had a great deal to give God thanks for, because He chose David to be prophet, priest and king, when everyone else either rejected or neglected Him. God protected David from being killed by King Saul who hunted Him fiercely. He allowed David not only to triumph over his enemies, but also to rest from them all for a season. So, David had many reasons to give thanks.

This collection of prayers and songs in the Psalms expresses the heartfelt feelings from deep within the Psalmists' souls. In them, we can read prayers of thanks for answered prayer, deliverance from difficulties, God's greatness, His protection, His enduring mercy, and never-ending love. God provides all of those things for us still today. So, the Prayers of Thanksgiving to God will always be relevant and necessary.

Prayer of Intercession

Coming from the word intercede – and intercede means going in on behalf of someone in difficulty or trouble - 1 Timothy 2: 1 says, *"Therefore I exhort first of all that supplications, prayers, intercessions, and giving of thanks be made for all men,"* Furthermore, James 5: 16 also reminds us, *"Confess your trespasses to one another, and pray for one another, that you may be healed. The effective, fervent prayer of a righteous man avails much."*

The Prayer of Intercession is also an expression of our love for our fellow man – that we would take the time to pray *for* others, even persons we do not know, and ask the Lord to direct their steps and help them through their time of difficulty or hardship keeps our hearts in right standing before the Lord.

Prayer of Petition & Counter-petition

To *petition,* as defined by the Oxford Living Dictionary, means *"A formal written request, typically one signed by many people, appealing to authority in respect of a particular cause; An appeal or request to a deity or a superior; Present a petition to (an authority) in respect of a particular cause."*

There is a time when the devil walks around looking for someone to go before the Lord about. Job 1: 6 – 12 tells us, *"Now there was a day when the sons of God came to present themselves before the Lord, and Satan also came among them. And the Lord said to Satan, "From where do you come?" So Satan answered the Lord and said, "From going to and fro on the earth, and from walking back and forth on it." Then the Lord said to Satan, "Have you considered My servant Job, that there is none like him on the earth, a blameless and upright man, one who fears God and shuns evil?" So Satan answered the Lord and said, "Does Job fear God for nothing? Have You not made a hedge around him, around his household, and around all that he has on every side? You have blessed the work of his hands, and his possessions have increased in the land. 11 But now, stretch out Your hand and touch all that he has, and he will surely curse You to Your face!" And the Lord said to Satan, "Behold, all that he has is in your power; only do not lay a hand on his person." So Satan went out from the presence of the Lord."*

There are several reasons the devil would seek to find specific ones to attack, including:

1. Our purpose, impact, faith in God, love for God and their commitment to God and the work of God.

2. The petitions of others to Satan to attack you, and the devil knows that he cannot attack us without going to God first to make his petition.

3. The Prophetic Word from God spoken over our lives.

Recognize that when God looks at us the enemy also looks at us trying to devise plans and petitioning God concerning us for permission to seek, kill and destroy.

Prayer of Supplication

In Philippians 4:6, we are told: *"Be careful for nothing; but in everything by prayer and supplication with thanksgiving let your requests be made known unto God."* The phrase, *"Be careful for nothing,"* literally means *"do not be anxious about/for anything."* Instead, in everything, every situation, we are to submit our requests to God through prayer and supplication with thanksgiving. We are to lift up our needs to the Lord – tell Him what our needs are and ask Him to supply them for us. This is our Heavenly Father inviting us to come to Him as the Elohim, so that He can show Himself strong to us as our El Shaddai – More Than Enough to us; Jehovah Jireh – our Provider; Jehovah Shalom – our Peace; Jehovah Rapha – our Healer; Jehovah Tsidkenu – our Righteousness, and everything we need on every level.

Spiritual Warfare Prayer

In Spiritual Warfare Prayer, you must pray with *bold authority, faith, obedience* and *knowledge of the Word of God*, because you are engaging in spiritual combat and the enemy knows the Word of God, knows the power of faith, knows the importance of obeying instructions in battle and knows when a person is functioning within or outside of their authority.

Matthew 18: 18 says, *"Assuredly, I say to you, whatever you bind on earth will be bound in heaven, and whatever you loose on earth will be loosed in heaven."*

This is the authority every believer in Jesus Christ has and must walk confidently in, so that we can lay hold of victories.

1 Timothy 1: 17 – 19 *"Now to the King eternal, immortal, invisible, to God who alone is wise, be honor and glory forever and ever. Amen. This charge I commit to you, son Timothy, according to the prophecies previously made concerning you, that by them you may wage the good warfare, having faith*

and a good conscience, which some having rejected, concerning the faith have suffered shipwreck"

Here we recognize that the moment God's prophetic word has been released over our lives, we become an even more visible target for the enemy. But know that God would not allow you to be more visible to the enemy if He didn't have a bigger plan of defeat for the enemy through you.

Prayer of Agreement

There is power in agreement. Matthew 18: 19 – 20 says, *"Again I say to you that if two of you agree on earth concerning anything that they ask, it will be done for them by My Father in heaven. For where two or three are gathered together in My name, I am there in the midst of them."*

Whenever we come into agreement with God's Word and His will in prayer, He will move mightily on our behalf. Growth and advancement take place when there is prayer of Agreement. (Acts 2; Acts 4). This is especially so between a wife and husband. The devil doesn't like agreement because it strengthens us spiritually and strengthens our faith in God which pleases God. Agreement concerning the things of God, the will of God and done in the Presence of God has the capacity to shatter the kingdom of darkness and cause us to walk in immense victory over sin, sickness, diseases and ultimately, over the enemy of our souls!

The Way To Pray

There is a wrong way to pray and a right way to pray; but it is not about the words we say but rather, about the state of our hearts as we pray. When we go before the Lord in Prayer of any kind, we must approach Him:

1. With reverence

2. In Humility of Heart and Spirit

3. Honestly (Don't try to pretend with God!)

Most importantly *be willing to spend time with God and avoid rushing.*

Recognize that the Heart is where the motives of the individual are formed and developed. The state of a person's heart influences/determines the spirit in which the person functions – the way we do something or say something and our actions and words have the capacity to either bring cleanse/bless or defile/curse. Look at Psalm 51: 10. If the motive isn't right it affects the spirit within which a person functions and makes decisions. It is why unforgiveness is so dangerous. This leads us to the Prayer of Repentance: Lord's Prayer.

The enemy enjoys the state of our heart and mind when we do not forgive, because it keeps us from experiencing the love and blessings of God and as such, weakens us spiritually. Make no mistake, the devil knows the Word of God too! He knows that Matthew 6: 14 – 15 says ""*For if you forgive men their trespasses, your heavenly Father will also forgive you. But if you do not forgive men their trespasses, neither will your Father forgive your trespasses."*

The Importance of Praying/Speaking In Tongues

Praying in the Holy Ghost or "praying in other tongues" accesses the communications network in the Spirit Realm – that invisible realm we cannot see in unless the Lord allows us that access. This communications network allows for conversation between the Lord and His saints – Spirit to spirit.

When we pray in other tongues, we are communicating in a supernatural language that gives us an upper hand on the forces of darkness and subsequently the upper hand in the spiritual warfare.

Oftentimes people are afraid to speak/pray in tongues – our heavenly language – because they do not understand it so they think it is nonsense. And as human beings, what do we do with anything that does not make sense to us? We reject

it, we criticize it, or we pretend it does not exist hoping it will go away. Sometimes we mock it, we rip it to shreds with our tongues and discredit it so that it is easier for us to reject it without remorse or guilt. We convince ourselves that anything that is different or that does not make sense to us is only worthy to be rejected. This is probably why many people reject God and His love, because He does not make sense to them, and they cannot comprehend Him – what He does or sometimes what His Word says, because oftentimes they do not seem logical.

So then, the "concept" of praying or speaking in tongues is a mindblower for many people – because they just cannot understand it.

1 Corinthians 14: 14 says, *"For if I pray in an unknown tongue, my spirit prays, but my understanding is unfruitful"*. That simply means that we will not understand the very things we are saying simply because spirit is speaking to spirit. Know this:

Here are some Truth Bombs:

1. God does not have to explain everything to us and He does not have to tell us all the details on any issue. He is God and He is Wisdom personified.

2. There are some things that the Lord will not allow us to understand.

Know that when you are speaking privately to God in your devotions, you will not necessarily understand what you are saying. That is a mystery. However, God may give the overall meaning. Recognize also that the only way we can effectively speak to angels is to speak in their language.

1 Corinthians 14: 1 – 4 is referring specifically to speaking in tongues publicly. The Scripture simply states that in pursuit of spiritual gifts, pursue the gift of prophecy more than you would speaking in tongues, because in

prophesying you edify everyone else letting them know what the Lord is saying to them. Speaking in tongues is speaking to God and speaking the mysteries of God. 1 Corinthians 14: 2 says *"For he who speaks in a tongue does not speak to men but to God, for no one understands him; however, in the spirit he speaks mysteries."*

According to Acts 1 and 2, when the Holy Spirit descended and the 120 were speaking in tongues, each of the 19 plus nations present heard the Apostles speaking their native tongue.

Recognize that speaking in tongues is one thing that identifies and, to an extent, unifies Christians.

When we see our own people of our own culture/nation/people, all formalities go. When that happens, we automatically begin to speak to them in the native tongue, with great relief and ease.

When we as citizens of heaven begin to speak the heavenly language, then other citizens of heaven know – that's one of us.

When we decree and declare something, we are stating what we want to happen for us on the earth. For example, *"I declare that every member of my household will give their hearts to the Lord and be saved within the next 6 months in the name of Jesus Christ of Nazareth!"* and they will serve the Lord for the rest of their lives.

However, when we want something from the heavens – a gift or supernatural finances, favor, grace, then we speak/pray in tongues.

Recognize that heaven does not operate on earthly currencies: it operates on *Grace, Favor, Faith, Gold* and *Silver*.

What the people of God did not have in the Old Testament was released in the New Testament at the Crucifixion, Resurrection and Ascension of Jesus Christ, and today we have access to those benefits. For example, in the time of the Old Testament the Holy Ghost would come upon certain ones seasonally; but now, He dwells in us and He gives us the opportunity to communicate with heaven directly and consistently.

The Early Church was so excited to have the Holy Spirit because they realized the heavenly communication was being restored; because it is a requirement for any citizen of any nation to speak that nation's language. (We cannot be a citizen of somewhere and not speak the nation's language.)

Adam, because of his fall in the Garden of Eden, lost the special communication between himself and God. Jesus – the 2nd "Adam" had to lay His life down and take it up again to restore the communication; hence Joel 2: 28. Jesus Christ had to die to fulfill Joel 2: 28 and establish Mark 16.

Recognize this: the Fear of the Lord must and will return to His House. We must be careful what we say about the Holy Spirit and His work. Speaking in tongues is the evidence that we have been baptized with the Holy Spirit. (If there is something we do not understand about the Holy Spirit, then we should not be so quick to rip it to shreds. Instead, we need to go to the Lord in prayer and ask Him to help us understand.

Gift of Diverse Tongues

This is what is called a *vocal gift* from the Holy Spirit. There are **three (3)** vocal gifts of the Holy Spirit:

1. *The Gift of Diverse Tongues*

2. *The Gift of Interpretation of Tongues*, and

3. *The Gift of Prophecy.*

With the Gift of Diverse Tongues is the supernatural utterance through the power of the Holy Spirit in a person that manifests as spiritual language. The Holy Spirit energizes the tongue to edify believers through language and music.

The Gift of Diverse Tongues is the most misunderstood and dynamic gift. It is not your prayer language, but it can surface through intercession, conference, or through the individual.

Diverse Tongues are Supernatural utterances in languages not known to or understood by the speaker. These languages may either be existent in the world, revived from some past culture, or "unknown" in the sense that they are a means of communication with God, that only He understands, and is inspired by the Holy Spirit (*Isaiah 28:11; Mark 16:17; Acts 2:4, 10:44-48, 19:1-7; I Corinthians 12:10, 13:1-3, 14:2, 4-22, 26-32*).

The Gift of Diverse Tongues is a spiritual gift involving ability to speak in foreign languages not previously studied by the speaker; or to respond to an experience of the Holy Spirit by uttering sounds for which there is no natural interpretation and could not be understood without the supernatural Gift of Interpretation. At Pentecost the church received the gift to communicate the gospel in foreign languages (*Acts 2*).

Definition of "*language*"

Britannica Encyclopedia defines *"language"* as *"a system of conventional spoken, manual, or written symbols by means of which human beings, as members of a social group and participants in its culture, express themselves. The functions of language include communication, the expression of identity, play, imaginative expression, and emotional release."*

In addition to this, based on what we can see in the Scriptures, and by *official* definition it is safe to say that languages represent nations, and make note that another term of the word *"language"* is *"tongue"*.

Citizens of Heaven

The moment you repented of your sins sincerely and accepted Jesus Christ as your Lord and Savior – the Lord of your life, and King of Heaven and Earth, He became your King and you became a citizen of heaven; (*and this is one reason the angels rejoice. Another reason is that you have embraced and accepted the pure sacrifice of the Blood of Jesus and the laying down of His life*) and God the Almighty King through the power of His Holy Spirit has been authorized to empower you with the language of Heaven!

So every Christian has dual citizenship! Earthly and Heavenly! (Being born in one country and being a citizen of another gives you the opportunity to know the language of your birth country, but you have to learn the language of your new country. So when we become Christians, we now have to learn our new language.)

Let's look at 1 Corinthians 13: 1 which says, *"Though I speak with the <u>tongues of men and of angels</u>, and have not charity, I am become as a sounding brass, or tinkling cymbal."*

We need to read the Word of God with understanding and recognize that every word and phrase has significance and meaning and not one word is wasted in the Bible. (One of the characteristics of the Holy Bible is that it is a Book of Mystery filled with clues.)

1 Corinthians 13: 1 is the beginning of a passage of Scripture that speaks about charity/love, yet within this one verse is hidden a significant clue concerning both the earthly and heavenly language. There are languages on the earth and there are also heavenly languages.

In addition to that, as we look at 1 Corinthians 14: 1 – 4 verse 2 says *"For he that speaks in an <u>unknown tongue speaks not to men, but to God</u>; for <u>no man understands him</u>; however, in the spirit he speaks mysteries."*

There is a language that angels and God understand according to 1 Corinthians 13: 1 and there is a language that only God understands according to 1 Corinthians 14: 2.

Citizenship and Language

As a citizen of any nation, you will need to know and speak the language of that nation/country. Why?

1. You will be able to effectively communicate with the other nationals so that there will be no misunderstanding, miscommunication and no division – so that there will be unity in the nation and that nation can stand and be a more effective unit – against the enemy at any level. So, a language not only represents a nation but it (potentially) unites the nation!

   In an article dated March 13, 2015, titled, **"A National Language Represents The National Identity Of A Country"** written by Asim Nawaz Abbassi, of Pakistan on www.yourcommonwealth.org he states, *"Indeed national language is a clear indicator that represents the national identity of a country. Language is a sensitive issue. It's also part of a nation and a person's heritage. To understand and penetrate deep into a community, one must be able to speak and understand the language of the community."*

   Additionally, in a survey report from the Pew Research Center titled **"Language: The Cornerstone Of National Identity"** dated February 1, 2017, it states, *"Majorities in each of the 14 countries polled say it is very important to speak the native language to be considered a true member of the nation..."*

Genesis 11: 1 says, *"Now the whole earth had one language and one speech."* Which, by the standards outlined before, tells us that they were citizens of a united earth.

2. To maintain the security of the people of the nation and to protect its borders, government and the various facets and industries of the nation. The nation needs to know if you are planning a conspiracy or overthrow; or if you are instigating division at any level because as the word says in Mark 3: 25 *"And if a house be divided against itself, that house cannot stand."* And that is something every enemy knows. The Divide and Conquer strategy is not only used where it concerns nations at war, but in business, in our personal lives and sadly, in the Church.

As citizens of heaven, we should never be afraid or ashamed of speaking our heavenly language – through it we harness our victories!

CHAPTER 6

Know The King's Ordinances

As Royal Daughters of the Most High God, Psalm 119 especially verses 97 – 105 are critical verses for us to know and use as our watchwords. That passage of Scripture says,

"Oh, how I love Your law! It is my meditation all the day. You, through Your commandments make me wiser than my enemies; For they are ever with me. I have more understanding than all my teachers, for Your testimonies are my meditation. I understand more than the ancients, because I keep Your precepts. I have restrained my feet from every evil way, that I may keep Your word. I have not departed from Your judgments, for You Yourself have taught me. How sweet are Your words to my taste, sweeter than honey to my mouth! Through Your precepts I get understanding; therefore I hate every false way. Your word is a lamp to my feet and a light to my path."

When we do not know what we are about, we operate in fear, insecurity, and rejection, because we do not feel confident in our capacity to achieve success and we do not feel we have what it takes. It is always a challenge to try to do something without knowing how to do it.

When you know the King's requirements, instructions, principles and laws, you can function with more confidence.

It is amazing how many of us as Christians are today living a life of powerlessness! Many of us have handed over our God-given authority to the devil with eyes wide shut! It is time to take back our authority!

Taking Authority

Galatians 5: 1 says, *"Stand fast therefore in the liberty by which Christ has made us free, and do not be entangled again with a yoke of bondage."*

The Word of God tells us in Matthew 28: 18 *"All authority has been given to Me in heaven and on earth."* Then Christ proceeds to extend this authority to us by giving us the Great Commission and told us to *"Go ..."*

The Lord further told us in the John 14: 12—14, *"Most assuredly, I say to you, he who believes in Me, the works that I do he will do also; and greater works than these he will do, because I will go to My Father...If you ask anything in My name, I will do it."*

I could continue quoting Scriptures to prove the kind of authority we have through Christ, but it comes back to one thing: in order to take back our authority, we must know the Word of God!

Pick up your Bible and turn to Mark 4: 35—41. Let's look at this Scripture—seriously!

Realize that the moment Christ determined that He wanted to cross over the other side, the winds arose.

Oftentimes, the moment we decide that we want more out of our Christian walk, more out of our relationship with God, then out of nowhere, come the things that the devil wants to use to confuse or discourage us! This "wind" causes the waves to arise and try to knock us off our feet and so we lose faith and oftentimes we feel as if we are sinking under the pressure!

Notice that when the disciples saw the storm and felt its effects, they became full of fear and empty of faith! Yet Christ was calm—in fact, He slept! They woke Him up, asking Him if He did not care that they were perishing! What a question to ask our Lord! Yet, we do it all the time! We often ask God, "God, don't you see what is going on? Are You really there?"

But look at what Christ did! He rebuked the wind and spoke to the sea! What the Lord is saying to us is that we must use the authority He has given us and rebuke Satan's activities and demons in the atmosphere (for Satan is the prince of the power of the air) and then declare that which we desire to see happen! Notice that the disciples and those around marveled at the fact that the winds and the sea obeyed Christ.

That tells us about the level of their faith and their view of their own authority and on God's ability to protect and help us!

We must be determined to walk in our Godly authority so that we can ultimately walk in victory! What is the level of your faith today? Are you walking in your authority? Take back your joy and your peace of mind! Take back our children from Satan's clutches, and your unsaved husband or wife, and live the abundant life that God has given you with the AUTHORITY He has given you! We are joint heirs with Christ!

The Devil Didn't Write Your Story

"Therefore we also, since we are surrounded by so great a cloud of witnesses, let us lay aside every weight, and the sin which so easily ensnares us, and let us run with endurance the race that is set before us, looking unto Jesus, the author and finisher of our faith, who for the joy that was set before Him endured the cross, despising the shame, and has sat down at the right hand of the throne of God." Hebrews 12: 1 – 2

For many who are determined to keep standing despite the circumstances, it feels like one of the most difficult and trying seasons yet! The devil has intensified his attacks and now he is trying to push all the buttons to cause you to fall into frustration, depression or anger in order to make you decree/say/confess things that are opposite to what God wants you to declare, believe, embrace and act on in this season!

The devil recognizes that something is just up ahead for you, and if he can get you to function according to his bidding and influence, then he will have you where he wants you functioning according to his will rather than the will of God!

We cannot ... no ... MUST NOT allow ourselves to react when the enemy pushes our buttons! People will say all kinds of unkind things to us in this season. Others will deliberately do things in order to get a certain response from us to satisfy their deep desire to see us be as miserable as they are inside! Jesus endured the cross as He stayed focused of the ultimate goal and greater joy- our salvation and eternal hope! Instead of reacting to all that distraction, and allowing just anything that comes to mind to exit our lips in response, let us exercise spiritual maturity this time around, and ignore the devil's weak attempts to resurrect the old us! Let us choose to stay focused and not miss a blessing!

Let us always keep this in mind, the devil did not write your story and he didn't write mine! He is a mere character in God's manuscript of our lives but we determine whether or not he has a speaking part in our lives! As the Word of God reminds us, it is GOD Who is the Author and Finisher of our faith!

It is God the Author Who writes all our stories and orchestrates events and causes paths to cross! He is God so He knows what the outcome of each event in our lives will be – or already is – He wrote it! Furthermore, because He is the Divine Playwright, we should always consult with Him on the parts we are not clear on, and trust that He knows what He is doing and what He wants to do with His characters – and HIS stories – our lives!

Keep in mind always, the devil did not write your story, God did – He is the Author and Finisher! Misery, fear, depression, frustration, hindrance of your blessings, sorrow, sadness, destruction and eternal death need NOT be your portion!

John 10: 10 – 11 reminds us, *"The thief does not come except to steal, and to kill, and to destroy. I have come that they may have life, and that they may have it more abundantly. I am the good shepherd. The good shepherd gives His life for the sheep."*

Furthermore, God is faithful to His Word and His promises, and He reminds us in Isaiah 55: 10 – 13, *""For as the rain comes down, and the snow from heaven, and do not return there, but water the earth, and make it bring forth and bud, that it may give seed to the sower and bread to the eater, so shall My word be that goes forth from My mouth; it shall not return to Me void, but it shall accomplish what I please, and it shall prosper in the thing for which I sent it. "For you shall go out with joy, and be led out with peace; the mountains and the hills shall break forth into singing before you, and all the trees of the field shall clap their hands. Instead of the thorn shall come up the cypress tree, and instead of the brier shall come up the myrtle tree; and it shall be to the Lord for a name, for an everlasting sign that shall not be cut off."*

Whatever the Lord says, He will do, but it is up to us to trust what He says, accept what He says as truth and to believe Him to the point where we are already thanking Him for the great things He will do and consider it already done!

Now it would also serve us well to remember that God is not only the Author but the Finisher – which means He refines the work! He does the fine-tuning of the manuscript and when He is done, nothing can change or tarnish it! He is of course, the Alpha and the Omega so everything starts and ends with Him and He always has the final say! He did say in Jeremiah 29: 11, *"For I know the thoughts that I think toward you, says the Lord, thoughts of peace and not of evil, to give you a future and a hope."*

Not only that – God is for YOU!!!!! If God is for you, who can be against you? Do you not remember that when God is with you, then there are more with you than are against you?

Keep standing and stay in God's presence! Do not react to the distractions! You are about to cross the threshold of God's promises for you! Do not let the enemy get a speaking part in your story and dictate a negative outcome! Stick to the Script God wrote for your life!

CHAPTER 7

Be Fearless And Faithful

The Word of the Lord has many examples of great women who didn't wear crowns, but who did great things in the sight of the Lord. They teach us many life lessons we can learn from on our journey being God's *Royalty In Motion*.

Jochebed

Jochebed was an Israelite born in Egypt and was the daughter of Levi, who was the son of the Levi who was Joseph's brother. Her husband Amram, was also of the tribe of Levi, and together they had three (3) children, Aaron and Moses and their sister Miriam. (Exodus 26: 59)

According to the book of Exodus, the Pharaoh at that time had decreed that all their baby boys were to be thrown into the Nile, because he feared that the Children of Israel might become too powerful. When Moses, her youngest child, was born, Jochebed hid him for three months until she could hide him no longer. To save her son's life, she made a wooden chest of bulrushes, made it watertight with slime and pitch and put the child in it. Fully aware that she (Jochebed) would not be able to protect Moses from the Pharaoh's cruelty, Jochebed placed Moses in a basket and released him in the flow of River Nile.

This is *Royalty In Motion* in action here – Resistance to sin, Determination, and Blind Faith. Jochebed did not yield to the sinful instructions to throw her son away as if his life had no value. She honored God by protecting him for as long as she physically could and then put Him in the hands of the Lord as she released Him into the Nile. She had no idea what would happen to her son or where he would end up. She did not even know if at the end of the day he would have been alive, but she knew she had to trust God completely and try her very best to protect and save him from the cruelty of Pharaoh and his evil instructions/decrees.

As a result of her faith, God caused the basket to be found by Pharaoh's daughter who was bathing in the river. The Lord knew that the Pharaoh's daughter was kind-hearted, and that she would be filled with love and compassion for the baby. So, He allowed her to find Moses and she decided to adopt him. Miriam, Moses' sister had followed the basket and came forward and offered to find a Hebrew woman to nurse the child for her. In what seemed to be Divine Wisdom, Miriam then brought her mother forward as the one who would nurse the child. Ultimately in the time where Pharaoh declared abortion and murder upon the Hebrew children – specifically the boys, because of His purpose for Moses and the determination and blind faith of His mother, Jochebed, He allowed Moses – the potential deliverer of the Hebrews Pharaoh enslaved, to be raised in Pharaoh's palace – raised like a king, while his own mother (unknown to Pharaoh and his daughter) got paid by them to raise Him for them! Who is like our God? What can't He do for, with or through you?

Mary (Martha's Sister)

Luke 10: 38 – 42 says, *"Now it happened as they went that He entered a certain village; and a certain woman named Martha welcomed Him into her house. <u>And she had a sister called Mary, who also sat at Jesus' feet and heard His word.</u> But Martha was distracted with much serving, and she approached Him and said, "Lord, do You not care that my sister has left me to serve alone? Therefore tell her to help me." And Jesus answered and said to her, "Martha, Martha, you are worried and troubled about many things. But one thing is needed, and <u>Mary has chosen that good part, which will not be taken away from her.</u>"*

Despite all that was happening around her, despite the fact that ordinarily she would be required to serve and be a good hostess to the very important guest they had with them – Jesus – Mary looked past all that and recognized the importance of being in His Presence, hearing what he had to say and learning all she could while He was with them. She discerned what was most important at that time and she was focused and determined to stay in His Presence. This must be a goal of Royalty In Motion, to ignore distractions, focus on staying in the Presence of the Lord and identify the opportunities to do so.

Mary Magdalene

Luke 8: 1 – 3says, *"Now it came to pass, afterward, that He went through every city and village, preaching and bringing the glad tidings of the kingdom of God. And the twelve were with Him, <u>and certain women who had been healed of evil spirits and infirmities—Mary called Magdalene, out of whom had come seven demons,</u> and Joanna the wife of Chuza, Herod's steward, and Susanna, and many others who provided for Him from their substance.*

Mary Magdalene was a woman who was demonically oppressed and in bondage, but she also had great love and compassion within her to express. Jesus had delivered her from the demonic oppression and she was eternally grateful to Him. She was very giving, a discerner, and one who loved the Lord very much. She was the same Mary who broke the jar of spikenard which was worth one year's wages, bowed at the feet of Jesus and poured the oil all over His feet and then proceeded to dry his feet with her hair. Humility, Genuine Love, Kind, Compassionate, and Willing to Give of Her Substance for a greater cause; does less talk and more action. These are qualities of a Queen – of *Royalty In Motion*.

Deborah

Deborah was a prophetess, a wife, and during the time of Israel's harsh oppression, she judged Israel. (Judges 4). She had a role in governing the affairs of the Children of Israel. She was the only female judge mentioned in the Bible.

Judges 4: 3 – 5 tells us, *"And the children of Israel cried out to the Lord; for Jabin had nine hundred chariots of iron, and for twenty years he had harshly oppressed the children of Israel. Now Deborah, a prophetess, the wife of Lapidoth, was judging Israel at that time. And she would sit under the palm tree of Deborah between Ramah and Bethel in the mountains of Ephraim. And the children of Israel came up to her for judgment."*

Judges during that time were chosen by God, each from a different tribe of Israel, (not voted in), and put in that position to rescue the people from their enemies and establish justice. The people would go to the judges to resolve conflicts and make judgements or counsel them. For as long as there were judges there was peace among the Children of Israel.

The Israelites were being oppressed by Jabin the king of Canaan, and the Lord instructed Barak, of the Naphtali tribe of Israel, to gather troops and deploy them against the king's army. In fear he did not obey, and Deborah called him in to tell him what the Lord told her to tell him. Judges 4: 6 – 9 *'Then she sent and called for Barak the son of Abinoam from Kedesh in Naphtali, and said to him, "Has not the Lord God of Israel commanded, "Go and deploy troops at Mount Tabor; take with you ten thousand men of the sons of Naphtali and of the sons of Zebulun; and against you I will deploy Sisera, the commander of Jabin's army, with his chariots and his multitude at the River Kishon; and I will deliver him into your hand'?" And Barak said to her, "If you will go with me, then I will go; but if you will not go with me, I will not go!" So she said, "I will surely go with you; nevertheless there will be no glory for you in the journey you are taking, for the Lord will sell Sisera into the hand of a woman." Then Deborah arose and went with Barak to Kedesh."*

Ultimately, Deborah was able to guide Barak through the instruction of the Lord into the victory.

Deborah was *Royalty In Motion*. She governed with authority, fearlessly willing to go up against the enemy of her nation at the instruction of God, because she was confident that God was with them and would be with them going up against the enemy based on His instructions to Barak. She was willing to follow the instruction of God where others were afraid to and God granted Israel victory through her guidance.

God allowed each of these women in their own time to come to the fore at a time where the men did not. Why didn't Amram as Jochebed's husband and head of the household the one to formulate and execute a plan to protect and save their son? They were both from the Tribe of Levi and of the same family and understood the significance of a son in the family. Why didn't Moses' father rise up and become more active in protecting and saving His son? Had he become complacent with the happenings of the time? Had he given in or given up hope when Pharaoh made the evil decree? Did he lose his zeal to resist the evils of the oppressive government that had enslaved them? Furthermore, it was not Aaron that followed after the basket, it was Miriam. Was Aaron learning from and copying the attitude of his father learning to simply yield to public opinion? If that is so, is that why he yielded to public opinion later in life and allowed a golden calf to be erected by the Children of Israel as they waited for Moses' return? Is this the complacency that Aaron learned from that caused him to be influenced by a sister who earlier in life had to step up to the plate and follow after her brother in a basket to ensure his safety?

Why was it that in a room filled with men who said they wanted to hear what Jesus had to say, that it was a woman who discerned and saw the value in Jesus, and washed and anointed His feet and used the hair on her own head, to dry His feet? Everything she did caused her to physically bow down to Him, staying at His feet, which indicated that she was completely yielded and submitted in her heart to Him, while there were many male spectators sitting around Him. They had various motives: some listening for Him to say something they could use against Him, some were waiting to see if they

really wanted to follow Him, and others, just wanted to see what the big deal was about with Jesus. But Mary Magdalene got a revelation of Who He was; after all, He delivered her from demonic oppression. She had an experience with Jesus that no one could take from her and in having that revelation, she knew nothing was too valuable to give to Him. The Scripture says that a woman's hair is her glory, and so, by using her hair to dry His feet, Mary Magdalene was symbolically submitting her glory to Him; she understood that her glory was nothing without and in the Presence of the Lord – her Lord. Ultimately, she became the first to see the risen Savior!

In a setting where the men were dominant, Mary (Martha's sister) sat among the men at the feet of Jesus to hear what He had to say. She was there in the midst of men which was not the "proper" thing to do then, but her focus was to embrace and accept the Word of God.

Why did Barak allow fear to influence his decision to obey God's instruction? Did he not understand that if God says He is going to allow you to do something, He already has everything in place to grant you the victory? Did Barak allow what he saw – the size and physical strength of the army to cause him to fear? Did he not remember the power of the Almighty God and His promise to keep Israel? As a result of his fear, it opened the way for a woman – Deborah – to rise up and take the reigns and guide them to victory where another woman was used to harness the ultimate victory by killing the head of the oppressive king's army.

Recognize that where men refuse or fail to come forward, God will use His Royal Daughters who are willing, and who choose faith over fear, to rise to the occasion and accomplish His will and purpose.

Each of these Royal Daughters had attributes of what it takes to be *Royalty In Motion* – in action for the King. As His Royal Daughters, we have the capacity to come out of our comfort zones, step up to the plate and move in faith along with the determination to succeed, great tenacity and the wisdom to obey the voice of God and His instructions and function where required – for our good and the good of our nation; and for His glory.

CHAPTER 8

Stay Focused! We Are The Salt Of The Earth

2 Kings 2:1 – 17 tells us that Elijah knew he was about to be taken up and as his protégé Elisha walked with him, the sons of the prophets questioned him concerning it several times. No doubt they must have either "seen" in the spiritual realm or had recognized that something was about to happen concerning Elijah that would affect Elisha. Nevertheless, each time they would come up to Elisha to point that out and start the gossip, he would promptly shut them up, shut down the conversation, and keep walking with His mentor and spiritual father. He chose to stay focused on the mission they were on so that he would not miss anything the that Lord was doing. Furthermore, at different points during the journey, Elijah would tell his protégé *"Stay here, please, for the Lord has sent me on to ..."* and every time he said that, Elisha would respond, *"As the Lord lives, and as your soul lives, I will not leave you!"*

This is the kind of focus and determination to finish the mission that we must employ as Royal Daughters because our Heavenly Father and King is depending on us to accomplish the mission He has downloaded in us. We should not be entertaining Gossip and Distractions; we must stay focused on doing the will of our Heavenly Father just as Jesus exemplified while He was on earth.

This is the time and season – the End Time – that the heavens are open and God is pouring out now, and we cannot afford to be distracted in any way because we do not want to miss what God is doing in us and for us so that He can use us – you and me – as vessels of Restoration. He wants to use you and me to:

1. Reach out and restore hope to those who have given up

2. Speak life into dead situations so that resurrection can come

3. Declare victory, healing and turnaround in the lives and situations of others

You did not go through everything you did for no reason. The enemy attacked but God, true to His Word, He turned it around for your good, and as a result, you are still here and still standing!

Despite the negative things the enemy is throwing in your direction, keep your hand in God's hand, stay in His Presence and keep walking with Him because He will not only bring you through it, but will cause you to have a testimony about His grace, goodness and mercy; and He will use you to reach, encourage and restore others to His honor and glory.

Now is the season to pursue God's presence without hesitation. This is the season to ask and it shall be given, to seek and you shall find, to knock and it shall be opened to you! God is specific in His instructions for a reason. He is specific in His Word and in His timing!

Royalty, it's time to go in to the King. Take the opportunity to enter the Presence of the King and make your requests known to Him.

Got Salt?

Matthew 5: 13 says, *"You are the salt of the earth; but if the salt loses its flavor, how shall it be seasoned? It is then good for nothing but to be thrown out and trampled underfoot by men."*

God's Word tells us that believers (in Him) are "the salt of the earth" and so, as Christians – as followers of Christ - we must recognize that in order to have its flavor, salt MUST go through one of two processes – Evaporation or Mining.

The Process of Evaporation

I learnt that the simplest method of evaporating brine is solar evaporation, but this can only be done in hot, dry, sunny places. The brine – the salt water from the ocean or salt lake – is collected into shallow ponds and allowed to evaporate in the sun.

The process of Evaporation means that it will go under the extreme heat of the sun and that heat is intensified because the brine is put in a shallow pool area so that evaporation takes place even faster. Further to that, while in the process of evaporation, the insoluble impurities – those things that will not dissolve away, will be revealed and literally pulled out of the salt. For example, sand, clay and slightly soluble impurities, such as calcium carbonate, settle to the bottom as evaporation begins. The brine is pumped or moved by gravity flow to another pond where calcium sulfate settles out as evaporation continues. The remaining brine is moved to yet another pond where the salt settles out as evaporation proceeds.

The Process of Mining

I also learnt that Rock Salt is mined from underground. Sometimes pressure from deep inside the Earth forces up large masses of rock salt to form salt domes. Once salt is detected, a drill is used to dig the area and dynamite placed in the holes. Then the area is blasted and the rocks of salt fall to the ground crushed. It is then collected/harvested and then brought in for further crushing. After that, the salt is separated by particle size, and there is further purification so that the non-salt elements are removed to ensure that pure salt remains.

Yield To The Process

If we are going to be the Salt of the Earth as the Jesus Christ has instructed us to be, then we must yield to the process He allows us to go through. There are some of us who will experience situations that are surface-level issues like protocol, how to deal with people at all levels, learning how to serve others well. The shallow pool the salt water is put in for processing is out in the open where anyone can view it, and that represents how publicly exposed God can allow our situations to be. But when the heat is added to the situation – when the situation intensifies, then our truths are revealed – our hearts, our attitudes, our fears, our weaknesses and our way of thinking. While all this is happening, many automatically begin to focus on the negatives we may see in the situation, and that is when we find out about our real selves. It is at that point the enemy of our souls capitalizes on this exposure and uses it to guilt us into running away from the process; but God is saying to us, "Focus on being the pure salt I am causing you to be." God is only allowing your 'insoluble impurities' to be revealed, not to embarrass or destroy you, but to allow you to see what exists within you that would hinder you fulfilling your purpose and to remove it from you (if you let Him) so that you can be pure salt for His use – to flavor the earth!

Interestingly, like the Rock Salt domes, there are those of us that God has to drill, dig and blast into – the hurt, the pain, the rejection, the loneliness, the hopelessness, the depression, the anger, the bad memories, the continual doubting of His voice, the breaking and scarring of our hearts, our deepest (untold) fears, the negative mindset and stubborn will we have, and He has to allow us to go through what seems like a dynamite field sometimes to get us to where He need us to be. Yet, even in all this, He is digging away at our hearts so that instead of a heart of stone – a hard heart, we have a heart of flesh that is pliable in His hands, and we learn how to love again and live again. He digs away at our fears and our mindsets to build our faith and confidence and to allow us to experience Him fully and deeply and be pliable in His hands so that our purpose is fulfilled. He is ultimately training us so that we will accomplish our earthly mission.

The salt has to be broken up – shattered to pieces - in order to be effectively used and to cover more ground. In Genesis 19: 26, Lot's wife became a pillar of salt, which means she became hardened, inactive, unusable and ultimately stuck in one place – frozen in the position of looking back. We cannot allow ourselves to become pillars of salt. If we keep looking back at the past and what we used to enjoy before the process began – if we do not let go of the old us, old mindset, old attitudes – then we are positioning ourselves to become ineffective, unprocessed and unable to be used by God, and as a result we are aborting our own purpose. We cannot look back and yearn for the old us and the old things when God is shaping a new and better you. If we become pillars of salt then we become hard and unusable and we will be left behind. **We need to be broken to be used**.

Instead of fighting Him on these things – instead of fighting with God through your processing/complaining about the process, He wants us to yield to the process He is allowing us to go through – because He knows what He is doing. It is through this process that our spiritual muscles are built and we develop our trust and faith in God – our All-Powerful, Omnipotent, Omniscient and Omnipresent God!

In 2 Samuel 22: 35 the Lord says, *"He teaches my hands to make war, so that my arms can bend a bow of bronze."* When we come up against resistance against our purpose, we must push back – with the

Word of God, and by following His instructions, allowing our spiritual muscles to be strengthened.

He says in Jeremiah 29: 11 – 13, *"For I know the thoughts that I think toward you, says the Lord, thoughts of peace and not of evil, to give you a future and a hope. Then you will call upon Me and go and pray to Me, and I will listen to you. And you will seek Me and find Me, when you search for Me with all your heart."* He knows how to get us to where He needs us to be for Him.

Ultimately, do not cease to *go*, *be*, and *do* for God our Creator, through Christ Jesus. You can do all things through Christ Who strengthens you (Philippians 4: 3). Remember that you are more than a conqueror through Him Who loved us (Romans 8: 37). Know that **all** things work together for good to them that love the Lord and are called according to HIS purpose! (Romans 8: 28)

So, while the process seems like it is breaking you down in every possible way, let it! Do not be afraid to be broken, because only then will the pure salt within you be revealed!

CHAPTER 9

The Attack On The Womb

Genesis 1: 26 – 28, "Then God said, "Let Us make man in Our image, according to Our likeness; let them have dominion over the fish of the sea, over the birds of the air, and over the cattle, over all the earth and over every creeping thing that creeps on the earth." So God created man in His own image; in the image of God He created him; male and female He created them. Then God blessed them, and God said to them, <u>"Be fruitful and multiply; fill the earth and subdue it; have dominion over the fish of the sea, over the birds of the air, and over every living thing that moves on the earth."</u>

Genesis 3: 13b – 15 "...The woman said, "The serpent deceived me, and I ate." So the Lord God said to the serpent: "Because you have done this, You are cursed more than all cattle, and more than every beast of the field; on your belly you shall go, and you shall eat dust all the days of your life. <u>And I will put enmity between you and the woman, and between your seed and her Seed; He shall bruise your head, and you shall bruise His heel."</u>

These two (2) scriptures are, to me, the central reasons for the attacks that the enemy of souls launches at women everywhere. The devil will always fight what God has ordained; even more so if what God has ordained has been empowered to fight and defeat/overcome the enemy of our souls. This should not, however, cause us to fear, but instead stir us into bold action and propel us to keep going for and in God to the place of our victory in Him! God has ordained us to be carriers of spiritually weaponized vessels that have the potential to defeat the enemy and destroy his plans.

In 2008, after our very painful experience, the Lord started speaking to me about the fragility of Life, how important it is for us to recognize that we are not here by chance or accident but that we each have a purpose. He continued to speak to me about the level of intense spiritual warfare that exists and surrounds our very birth and existence. He allowed me to see the fact that many women go through very painful experiences –such as the loss of a child whether before or after birth, and that these experiences hit hard at many women's self-esteem/self-confidence as well as their emotional and mental health. It is real and serious. He also allowed me to understand that it does not stop with women, but that it affects their husbands, their children (if any at that time), the grandparents – entire families are affected when such life-changing events happen. Something like this becomes a turning point for many families. Many families fall apart after a loss like that, very few grow closer.

Then the Lord began to reveal to me that as women, we have been blessed with the capacity to impact the lives and positively influence the lives of the people around us and even on nations – another reason the fight is so intense. It was upon that realization that the Lord helped me understand that we go through issues like these because of what we represent – a reminder to the enemy of his ultimate defeat.

Recognize that the devil does not fight you because you are weak, he fights you because of the greatness, strength and capacity to overcome that God has put in you. He is afraid you will realize what God has placed within you: the capacity to carry and bring to birth the embodiment of his defeat. He is afraid you will find out who you really are and the defeated foe he really is. He is afraid you will recognize that through Jesus Christ the King of Kings and Lord of Lords, you have the power and *the authority* to conquer and overcome everything he throws at you, so that you walk in true victory and liberty!

There are many today who are going through daily life not knowing how priceless and valuable they are to the world and to God. Every person reading this right now, every person born in this world has been *"fearfully and wonderfully made."* (Psalm 139: 14). It means God took great care in creating you to be that uncommon individual with supernatural weaponry, having a special, unique, Divine connection, embedded with Divine instructions, carefully thought out and purposed by the Creator – a unique design – loaded with gifts and talents and granted new mercies and benefits daily so that you fulfill your purpose, manifest your potential and make a difference in the world for Him! It is time for you to activate what God has put within you and fulfill your purpose.

Women, too often we compete and compare ourselves with others when we should be embracing our own difference, and complementing each other with our gifts and talents and realize our potential – make a difference in the lives of those around us so that we can live the best life for the glory of our King!

The Hidden Agenda

As women, we are up against not only the spiritual warfare, but there is a hidden agenda on the natural level that we need to be aware of and be ready to fight and win.

The devil's goal is to destroy what we call the Traditional Family Structure – that is – husband, wife and children. Recognize that according to Genesis 1: 27 – 28 and Genesis 2: 24 this is what God wants and has ordained.

In her book, *Stand for the Family*, Sharon Slater – President of Family Watch International, stated, *"...It is not just one person, group, law, policy or movement that is the root cause of the breakdown of the family. Rather, there are multiple forces that, when combined, are having a devastating impact."*

The enemy's goal is to weaken the family. There are high level authorities in the various nations and highly influential, international institutions whose goals are to promote everything that opposes the Divinely-ordained family structure.

Further to this, there are "radical feminists" whose goals are to remove men from their God-ordained leadership roles in the home and instead be the ones to lead in that capacity.

Know that "radical feminists", according to author and activist Sharon Slater (*Stand for the Family*), are not "*...women who are working to further the legitimate rights of women.*" But are those "*...women who espouse a militant, anti-patriarchal ideology that all men oppress women and who work to legalize abortion and to promote lesbian, transgender and homosexual rights, among other things*".

That is everything that goes **against** the principles, instructions and Word of God, and as women, we need to be aware of what is happening in our society and in our world so that we can strategically position ourselves spiritually and naturally to defeat the enemy. The Family is where that victory begins.

Head of the Household

The truth is that being the head of a household is more than just making major decisions for the other members of the family unit. Being the head of the household comes with the Spiritual, God-ordained authority to do so and that was already given to the males of our species by God (Genesis 1) We cannot do to change that; not even a gender change.

What we as women must seek to do, however, is to have a strong, healthy relationship with God through Jesus Christ, and allow Him to reveal who He needs us to be as women in and for our families, communities and the nations. We must allow Him to show us the purpose for which we were created – individually and collectively – and show us how to function and fight, even at the natural level. We fight, not carnally, but with Divine wisdom, so that we can help to effectively empower other women – our daughters and sisters – and strengthen the hands of the kings in our lives, so that together we will ultimately defeat the enemy of souls.

In addition to this, we must pray for, support, encourage and stand with the head (?) and the high priest of the home – the husbands God has given us as women, and we must pray for and together with our husbands, to direct, provide for and cover our family, so that together we can accomplish the will of God and defeat the enemy.

This is one of the reasons it is so important for us to allow the Lord to choose the husband He has for us, so that, through the union, He can create the husband and wife power team He needs to possess lands, be fruitful, multiply, replenish the earth, build the Kingdom and live the life.

Remember that God knows why He created us, and what He wants to accomplish through us and He knows how it needs to be done. Our obedience is key to our victory and a life of true prosperity.

The Feminine Issues

More and more women throughout the globe today are going through very serious health issues and a great deal of it is concentrated on the reproductive system. The attack is on against women carrying and bringing forth the God-given seed and producing the fruit of the womb to do according to Genesis 3: 15. The support and promotion of abortion, same-sex relationships, masturbation, promiscuity and use of adult "toys" and stimulants are tools the enemy uses to attack women's reproductive system. Ultimately, those things are contrary to God's instruction to man in Genesis 1: 28, which says, *"Then God blessed them, and God said to them, "Be fruitful and multiply; fill the earth and subdue it; have dominion over the fish of the sea, over the birds of the air, and over every living thing that moves on the earth.""*

Furthermore, the witchcraft, sexual immorality and sexual perversion and un-Godly practices are all on the rise and add to the evil concoction of activities attacking the womb. There are many women who engage in witchcraft to stop wives from conceiving for their husbands because they want those husbands to come to them instead. It is not an opinion or fallacy, it is real! Other women carry out witchcraft to stop the man from having any desires for his wife and instead desire them. There are men who engage witchcraft and other un-Godly activities to help them "perform" better and longer in the bedroom. However, all that can manifest into physical and spiritual attacks affecting all involved.

The Physical Manifestations

Mark 5: 25 – 32 tells us, "<u>Now a certain woman had a flow of blood for twelve years, and had suffered many things from many physicians.</u> *She had spent all that she had and was no better, but rather grew worse. When she heard about Jesus, she came behind Him in the crowd and touched His garment. For she said, "If only I may touch His clothes, I shall be made well." Immediately the fountain of her blood was dried up, and she felt in her body that she was healed of the affliction. And Jesus, immediately knowing in*

Himself that power had gone out of Him, turned around in the crowd and said, "Who touched My clothes?" But His disciples said to Him, "You see the multitude thronging You, and You say, 'Who touched Me?'" And He looked around to see her who had done this thing. But the woman, fearing and trembling, knowing what had happened to her, came and fell down before Him and told Him the whole truth. And He said to her, "<u>Daughter</u>, your faith has made you well. Go in peace, and be healed of your affliction."

This Scripture helps us to recognize several things.

1. This was possibly a gynecological issue that this woman was dealing with, and many, (including herself and the physicians of her time), did not understand nor could they explain what was happening. But remember too that while the technology we have today did not exist then, they could have and should have sought the Lord – the Great Physician for answers, as was done in 2 Kings 20: 1 – 11.

2. Faith is required for healing and healing of gynecological issues is possible. The passage of time does not make healing less relevant or less possible – our faith in God's capacity to grant us healing is a significant part of the process.

3. Not only did the woman lift her faith and believe in the healing power of Jesus Christ, but in addition to that, she acted on her faith by reaching out to the One she believed was the Source of her healing and subsequent victory over this grave issue. Furthermore, she strategically positioned herself in the throng of the crowd where she thought she

could hide while she reached out earnestly, desperately to receive her healing. When Jesus asked the questions, "Who touched My clothes?" and "Who touched Me?" she could have run away in fear and kept silent about it because she was healed instantly. But she came forward, admitted to her action publicly and as a result, Jesus identified her as *"Daughter."*

Today, many women suffer greatly with gynecological issues. There is a significant increase in the number and types of reproductive issues in women especially compared to 20, 30, 50 years ago. Technology has also increased, so more information about these issues are more and more accessible.

There is, however, significant increase in the amount of processed foods and convenience foods we eat as we "progress" on this planet.

What I share below is information that I have gathered from online research and direct conversations with doctors. Please note that I am not a medical professional, and as such I am not in any way giving medical advice here. I am simply sharing information I have gathered in an effort to make us more aware. Please seek medical advice from the medical professionals.

Many women suffer from issues such as:

Endometriosis

Under normal circumstances, after the egg is fertilized, it travels through the Fallopian Tubes, and is implanted in the wall of the uterus and grows. Endometriosis is a problem affecting a woman's uterus—the place where a baby grows when a woman is pregnant. Endometriosis occurs when the kind of tissue that normally lines the uterus grows somewhere else. It can grow on the ovaries, behind the uterus, on the bowels, or on the bladder. Rarely, it grows in other parts of the body.

This "misplaced" tissue can cause pain, infertility, and very heavy periods. The pain is usually in the abdomen, lower back, or pelvic areas. Some women have no symptoms at all, and having trouble getting pregnant may be the first sign they have endometriosis.

Uterine Fibroids

Uterine fibroids are the most common noncancerous tumors in women of childbearing age. Fibroids are made of muscle cells and other tissues that grow in and around the wall of the uterus, or womb. Fibroids can grow on the inside or on the outside of the womb itself.

Dr. Yvonne Munroe-Whitmore, MD shared with me that *"Fibroids inside the womb itself occupy some of the space where the baby should be and so it causes a problem during the pregnancy for the mother. They can obstruct the baby passing through the (birth) canal at the time of birth. If it blocks the entrance near the cervix, then at the time of birth the baby can't pass through. On the other hand, fibroids on the outside of the womb then they won't pose such a big problem for the baby."* So, the location of the fibroids determines a great deal in terms of what happens with the mother and child throughout the entire pregnancy and at the time of birthing. Additionally, being pregnant while having fibroids is extremely painful for the woman.

Dr. Munroe-Whitmore continued to share that, *"Where the fibroids are on the outside of the womb, they can press on the bladder and cause us to urinate very often; or they can press on the intestines, blocking bowel movement from the body, and cause even greater problems."* Ultimately, fibroids can obstruct any area of the abdominal cavity and cause significant problems for the woman.

From a spiritual perspective, we need to recognize that the enemy's goal in this is to either stop the woman becoming pregnant to bring forth a child, or to stop the growth and birthing of the vessel God is preparing to defeat him – "bruise his head". (Genesis 3: 15). Knowing these things help us determine how to pray for victory over this issue.

The cause of fibroids is unknown. Scientific Research states that African-American women carry the highest risk of having them. It also states that in general, women who are overweight have a higher risk of having fibroids.

The symptoms of fibroids include:

1. Heavy or painful periods or bleeding between periods.
2. Feeling "full" in the lower abdomen.
3. Urinating often.
4. Pain during sex.
5. Lower back pain.
6. Reproductive problems, (*Infertility, Multiple Miscarriages, or Early Labor*)

But some women will have no symptoms.

Urinary Tract Infection (UTI)

This is very common among women. A urinary tract infection (UTI) is an infection in any part of your urinary system — your kidneys, ureters, bladder and urethra. Most infections involve the lower urinary tract — the bladder and the urethra.

Women are at greater risk of developing a UTI than men. Infection limited to your bladder can be painful and annoying. However, serious consequences can occur if a UTI spreads to your kidneys.

Gynecologic Cancer

Gynecologic cancer is any cancer that starts in a woman's reproductive organs. Gynecologic cancers begin in different places within a woman's pelvis, which is the area below the stomach and in between the hip bones. For example:

1. Cervical cancer
2. Ovarian cancer
3. Uterine cancer
4. Vaginal cancer
5. Vulvar cancer

These are the most common gynecological cancers today.

Knowledge is key, and when we know what we are dealing with, then we can know how to fight but not only on the natural level, we can fight on the spiritual level as well, because we will know what to pray for specifically. Dr. Simone Van Horn, MD said, *"Cervical Cancer has seen some increase, only because women have been more educated on the need for pap smears which causes detection earlier. There has been a greater emphasis on women's health and trying to prevent these cancers from initiating, but the emphasis also causes more diagnoses to be made, and more are made earlier to prevent death."* Imagine what we could do if we added Spiritual Warfare Prayer to the equation!

Dr. Yvonne Whitmore, MD, shared that, *"Cervical cancer is quite common and almost all cervical cancers are caused by a common virus called the Human Papillomavirus or HPV."* She said that some HPV types can cause changes on a woman's cervix that can lead to cervical cancer over time, while other types can cause genital or skin warts. Furthermore, smoking, having HIV, using birth control pills for five or more years, having three (3) or more children, and having several sexual partners are just some factors that increase a woman's risk of having Cervical Cancer.

Other diseases affecting a woman's reproductive system include:

1. HIV (Human Immunodeficiency Virus) and AIDS (Acquired Immunodeficiency Syndrome)
2. Interstitial Cystitis
3. Polycystic Ovary Syndrome (PCOS)
4. Sexually Transmitted Diseases (STDs)
5. Sexual Violence
6. Intimate Partner Violence (IPV)

When we understand what takes place in a woman's body, especially regarding her entire reproductive system – and in particular, the womb – then we will know how to pray for victory and how to fight the Spiritual Warfare needed to defeat the enemy. This is what the enemy does not want and this is exactly what we need to do. The fight is real, but God desires to empower us spiritually and naturally, so we can be victorious in every area of our lives and by extension our families, communities and nation can be as well.

Take Care of Your General Health

Please take care of your health, because good health is invaluable. These issues, in addition to fatigue and stress are enemies to conception. The enemy is determined to continually attack the womb. We need to be even more determined to fight back, because God has equipped us to do so and is ready to empower and activate His Royal Daughters to walk in victory over infirmities. Many of us,

especially those who are mothers, there is a big part of us that takes care of everybody else first and leave ourselves for last in many cases. We see to it that our children eat even if we do not. We feed our children and husbands what is healthy, we ensure that as far as is possible for us, they have what they need; then we take what is left. We hurriedly eat the junk so that we will have the time to prepare food for everybody else. By the time we are done preparing breakfasts, lunches and dinners, and carrying out daily activities, we have just enough physical strength to barely say "Goodnight!" We do not eat the way we should to promote good health. We do not exercise the way we should because we have no time to do that. We do not take supplements or have the fruits, vegetables and juices we need to keep us going the way God intended and it is to our detriment.

If we are sick, we cannot function effectively – physically nor spiritually; nor can we fulfill our purpose. If we are unwell it affects our family, threatens our jobs and hinders us from fulfilling our purpose. Our husbands, children and other relatives are negatively affected and we run the risk of not reaching those we need to reach for God. Imagine waiting on help to save your life/soul and it is not coming because the one who is to help you is sick and unable to come to your aid.

As you function in your various roles daily, women, take care of you – not instead of your family, but in addition to your family.

1. Get your medical check-ups regularly.

2. Find a good Primary Care Physician you can actually talk to, who will attentively listen to you express your issues.

3. Find a good gynecologist you can trust.

4. Drink more water daily – add lemon juice for good measure. (From a real lemon you cut)

5. Eat healthy foods – balanced meals, real juices, and sit with your family to do so as far as is possible for you.

6. Exercise daily – walk, jog or do some aerobics in your living room. (Running the kids around the house does not cut it.)

7. Go to the bathroom when you need to – **do not** practice to "hold it in". Your health is important – it is one of your biggest assets.

Those are just the basic things.

At the end of the day, from the global LGBTQ (Lesbian, Gay, Bisexual, Transgender, and Queer) agenda, to the continuing increase in the fight to legalize Abortion, the push for Population Control, the radical feminists' anti-patriarchal agenda for the global society as well as the push to sexualize children through the education system and national laws – there is a real fight against the womb and the fruit of the womb. Every time a child is born it is a reminder to the enemy of souls that there is another soul coming forth to see to his defeat – one more who shall bruise his head.

CHAPTER 10

Be Poised And Positioned For Greater

The King of Kings wants His Royal Daughters to be at the place in Him, in His will for us, poised and in position to S.O.A.R. in Him, through Him, for Him. He has great plans for each of us – plans so much more immense, intense, more far-reaching than anything we could imagine. Plans that are so big that only the resources of the Limitless and Almighty God can get it accomplished.

Poised and Positioned to S.O.A.R.

As a child, I enjoyed listening to the beauty pageants aired on the radio. They were not aired on television then, so we could only imagine, by the announcer's descriptions, what the entrants must have looked like, how they walked, how stately they must have looked. But there was one word I would hear the announcers use to describe some of the women as they strutted down the runway before the judges, and that word never left me. I also noticed that the women they described with that word always ended up in the top ten (10). That word was *"poised"*.

Poised

According to the Oxford Dictionary, the word *"poised"* means, *"having a composed and self-assured manner. Having a graceful and elegant bearing."*

The Royal Daughter of the King of all Kings, must embody a certain level of composure (remaining calm in high-stress situations) self-confidence, grace and elegance. The Royal Daughter of the King of Kings must carry herself with calm confidence, polish and sophistication as she represents her Father and King.

When many women hear the words *"polish"* and *"sophistication"* they mentally "throw in the towel" their hearts sink and self-confidence plummets, and words such as *"stuck up, snobbish, unworthy, not good enough, or rich,"* immediately come to mind followed by. **Stop right there!**

Sophistication, elegance, grace and polish are words no woman should ever be afraid of or afraid to be. These words are not about your clothes; it's about your character. Neither is it about where you are from, what you did in the past, where you are now (spiritually or naturally), who your parents are, your family name, the color of your skin, nor your race – it is about WHOSE you are and about WHOM you choose to serve. The moment you embrace the truth of God's Word, Jesus Christ the Risen Lord as Savior, then you have begun to accept your Royal heritage. Like Esther, you will begin to recognize the significance of your purpose and calling, and its place in the fulfillment of God's plan for mankind. The devil does not want you to know who you are and the authority you have in God, and it is *our responsibility* to be all God says we are to be for Him in this life.

I believe initially, Esther did not *feel* like a queen – but she was a queen all along. It was when she truly embraced her purpose, she saw that she was called to save a people, a nation and not simply there to enjoy her position as queen for herself. Imagine her thoughts as Mordecai, her mentor, told her – an orphan raised by her male cousin – that she was to enter the pageant of women from all across the province where the one woman would be selected to be the wife of the king!

Let us not allow our self-confidence fly through the window. Remember that you are fearfully and wonderfully made by the Creator of all mankind, and you have purpose and potential.

Sophistication is not about pride. The word means *"the process or result of becoming cultured, knowledgeable"*. You learn, or are put in a position to learn about things beyond your own environment or scope on a daily basis. Always be willing to learn wherever you go, from the greatest to the least. You can learn from an ant; you can learn from the leader of a nation; you can learn from a prisoner; you can learn from the wealthy; you can learn from the poor; you can learn from the homeless; you can learn from a child.

In addition to this, the Holy Spirit of God is an Excellent Teacher and can teach you anything, and with anything. God can open doors of access for you anywhere He chooses and cause you to excel. But it is our willingness to learn and go through the processes involved in learning that will take us into the *"greater"* that God has for us.

Positioned

The word *"positioned"* comes from the word *position*, and it means *"bodily posture, attitude; mental attitude"*. When the Lord says we are to be positioned for greater, recognize that positioning first takes place in the mind. That is why the Lord tells us not to be conformed to this world but to be transformed by the renewing of our minds. As such, what the Lord wants us to do in this season is to renew our minds, be open to His brand of change, and ensure that our mental attitude toward Him, His Word, and how He moves or will move is flexible so that we are willing to embrace what we see Him do. He also wants to go through the doors of opportunity and access that He will open for us going forward in supernatural and uncommon ways.

Our Creator knows every plan for us and thought He has toward us and it is all good! (Jeremiah 29: 11; Psalm 139). He, therefore knows how to position us. That being said, the Lord wants His Royal Daughters to be ready for what He is about to do. We are now seeing on a global level, that women are coming to the fore in all areas like never before – in government, ministry, business, education, finance, entertainment – every major facet of society throughout the globe. In countries where women were once treated as chattel, unrecognized by their own government, after years of resistance they are now being allowed the right to vote, which means the state/government has to recognize them.

There is a great deal that God has deposited in us as women and the Lord wants to use us to bring change in all these areas and make a significant difference. The question is, are we coming to the fore as Jezebels (*1 King 16 – 21; 2 Kings 9; Revelation 2: 20*), Delilahs (*Judges 16*) and Vashtis (*Esther 1*); or are we going to come forward as the Esthers (*Esther 1 – 10*), Ruths (*Ruth 1 – 4*), Huldahs (*2 Kings 22: 13 – 15; 2 Chronicles 34: 21 – 28*), and Annas (*Luke 2: 36-38*) that God has created us to be. How we manage the resources, gifts, talents and opportunities God grants us, and how we treat Him, His people, our calling and our purpose will determine the level our success and comprehensive prosperity we achieve.

Recognize that it is important to wait on the Lord for what He wants to do in your life. Some are so eager to be married without even realizing what it all entails, not recognizing that it is not about "making it official" so you are not counted as a fornicator. It is not about getting together officially so that you can engage in the wonderful, highly intimate benefits. When God allows the man to find his wife – the bone of his bone and flesh of his flesh, He has something extremely uncommon, special, unique and unstoppable in His plans for that unit as long as they function in His will and obey His instructions to and for them.

Positioning for Leadership

In Exodus 2: 1 – 10, the entire story of Moses' start in life is about Divine Positioning!

At the time Moses was born it was terrible for the Children of Israel because the Pharaoh had ordered the killing Hebrew boy babies – selective partial birth abortions; and Moses' mother had to hide him and then give him away. He was subsequently found by Pharaoh's daughter who raised him in Pharaoh's palace. God used an unusual method to get into the inner workings of the Administration, so that when the appointed time came, Moses could speak from a position of authority and knowledge.

The time of Moses was a time of great oppression against God's people. The order had been given for the newborn Hebrew boys to be killed in an effort to control the population growth of the Hebrews to keep them in slavery/oppression. Moses' mother kept and hid him for 3 months after he was born and then *"...she took an ark of bulrushes for him, daubed it with asphalt and pitch, put the child in it, and laid it in the reeds by the river's bank."* (Exodus 2: 3) She sent her son out by faith not knowing what would happen to him. I can imagine she must have hoped that he would be found by someone who would take pity on him, save him and raise him.

His big sister followed his basket as it travelled on the river, to see where he would end up. Pharaoh's daughter went out to bathe in the river and found him. She fell in love with the baby Moses and his big sister used the opportunity to she offered to find 'a Hebrew woman' to nurse the baby for her. Pharaoh's daughter agreed and instructed that she would pay the nurse to do it; and big sister went and called their own mother to be the nurse.

So not only did God allow this child to be saved, but his own mother got paid to be his mother – something she would have done for free under normal circumstance. God allowed the oppressors of the Hebrews – His chosen people, to fund and feed His people during the time of slavery and oppression.

Despite their determination to maintain their oppressive hold on the Children of Israel through population control and by giving the orders that the newborn Hebrew sons should be killed at birth, (in other words he passed the abortion law); God allowed the daughter of the king who passed that law to save one of them, and pay his mother to play her natural role and raise him in the house of the king who gave the order! What an amazing God!

God positioned Moses, his sister Miriam, and his mother Jochebed, and that entire household, and allowed Moses to be raised in the palace of the oppressive king, so that He could use Moses to deliver Israel from oppression and save a people/a nation, to bring them from bondage to freedom.

One of things the Lord wants us to remember is that He has the power and the authority to cause every adversity that was supposed to kill you, to work for your good! He simply needs us to trust Him to do it for us. He is positioning you to use you for greater things. Do not complain about your adversity, because the Lord can let it become the springboard from which we soar! We can either choose to focus on everything that affects us negatively and whine and complain about it, talking about how disadvantaged you are; or, you can choose to look at the bigger picture and how God orchestrated everything to deliberately cause you to be here right now, and the fact that the enemy did not win and that now you are poised and positioned to accomplish greater.

Make this declaration: "**Everything I have experienced, that was meant to destroy me did not! God used it to position me for what He is about to use me to do for Him – through Him! I am positioned to SOAR!**"

Recognize this: Your story – all your adversities, issues, problems, extremely painful circumstances – they became your training ground. They were also your camouflage. Through this, God allowed you to be discounted and underestimated by those around you – those who saw you in your mess, those who did not see you as anyone significant and who ignored you and even your cries for help – even family members. All that, brought you to this place – where you are stronger, wiser, and more determined than ever to succeed; and if God can take you to this place, then He can take you from here into greater.

Positioning for Promotion and Prosperity

Under Naomi's mentorship, Ruth was being positioned for greatness! It meant following the instructions of her mentor and serving her by submitting to her leadership.

There is one thing we should recognize about a mentor. The Lord is the One Who aligns you with your mentor based on what

His purpose is for your life. You must ask the Lord which direction to go in identifying your mentor. A mentor is one who has gone through some real-life challenges and has overcome and/or learned some valuable lessons from those experiences. He/She has that level of spiritual, emotional and mental maturity to impart to his/her protégé without being jealous of that protégé, or without having an ulterior motive to milk the protégé, and to ultimately unlock their potential and help them to fulfill their purpose. The mentor walks in integrity and will help their protégé to do the same. God allows the mentor to go through many challenges and overcome, and if the protégé follows the instructions he/she receive from his/her mentor, then they will receive the benefits and blessings that the mentor received without having to walk the road himself/herself.

Remember this, a mentor is not your friend to tell you what you want to hear, but instead what you *need* to hear. We either learn by mistake or mentorship.

Naomi knew what it was like and what it cost to shift out of position and away from the will of God, because she went through it with her husband Elimelech.   (Interestingly Elimelech's name means "God his King."). That shift outside the will of God for their lives caused Elimelech to die outside of his place of blessing and sustenance – outside of Bethlehem, which means "the House of Bread". He died in a place of lack and no identity because Moab means "Who is your father". He shifted from a place where his Father was King, and because He did not trust God enough to take Him through the famine. Furthermore not only was the head and high priest of the home cut down, but it cost the family two (2) sons as well, that would have carried on the family name as well as the continuation of the lineage, because they each died childless; and it cost Naomi her entire family and she became bitter *Nevertheless*, God still allowed the connection between Naomi and Ruth; an unbreakable loyalty between them that:

1. allowed them to stay connected at their lowest point,

2. allowed Naomi to mentor Ruth and teach her to position herself for redemption, and

3. caused them to experience elevation and turn around to fulfill a bigger purpose – the ultimate birth of David who became king, through whose lineage came Jesus the ultimate Redeemer! So, they were positioned to become Royalty!

Remember David. He was the ignored one among seven (7) other brothers and was regarded as the least of the lot. Yet God allowed him to be camouflaged under all that ruggedness and rejection, camouflaged out in the field with the sheep and wolves and bears, meanwhile he was being trained to become the kind of king who knew how to deal with the kind of enemies he would face in the future. He was being trained in the field to be a hunter and learn how to protect what would be considered prey – so that he would know how to deal with a king and a father-figure that would constantly hunt him and still remain faithful to God in the midst of it!

Remember Abraham, who was instructed to leave his father's house and everything he had been accustomed to, brought through many lands leading many, told he would be father of many nations at a time when he and his wife was past the normal child-bearing stage in life and had no children at the time, who had to endure the betrayal of a nephew – Lot, who felt he had to pretend to be his wife's brother in order to save his own skin from death, and had to watch her being admired and taken into the palace of a king who had the authority to take his life in an instant; who had to offer up for sacrifice the very son that God had promised him, but who also passed that test thereby saving his son. God used all Abraham's experiences, struggles, disappointments and joys to pave the way for a people to come forth and bring hope to many of us today!

Understand, therefore, that positioning begins in your mind, so how you think - your mindset - determines whether or not you take up your position and soar!

1. Make use of the resources around you to help you get in position. There is a reason God has allowed you to be able to access different resources in different seasons.

2. Start cleaning up your credit and position yourself to be a land-possessor. It is ordained for you to own property and not just to say you own it. If you do not own property, you do not have a say.

3. Get your drivers' license and position yourself not only to own a vehicle or vehicles, but also to move when God says and go where He says.

4. Learn protocol, cultures and languages where you can and engage in them, and position yourself to be used by God in different nations or among different peoples. If you are part of a vision that is international, why do you know only one language or culture?

Positioning for Leadership

Positioning does not begin when a person is promoted or elevated, and this is what many people do not understand. When God is positioning us, we do not have a say in how He chooses or should choose to do it, or what strategies/methods He should use to get us to the place He needs us to be.

When we are being prepared or positioned in life and ministry God's way, then contrary to the way in which the world operates, our only roles are to:

1. Follow the instructions of the Lord, and

2. Trust Him completely

That is often easier to say than to do, but it is not impossible and absolutely necessary.

There are many whom God has aligned for positioning but the moment they sense or are able to see or catch a glimpse of what they think they know the next move God is going to make concerning them, they become impatient and everything that is within their hearts are revealed. They begin to feel that they know all that they need to know and that they can handle it all now. Some may even say they can handle it better than those set over them, and they begin to think that they should be elevated, promoted or released immediately to do what they believe God wants them to do NOW, and that anything else means that man – their leader/mentor - is holding them back.

Strategy:

Recognize that what we as leaders/visionaries/mentors are there to teach and to give direction and guidance, particularly from a Biblical perspective, to those under our care/training. GOD IS THE ONE WHO DOES THE BREAKING AND FIXING! We need to stop asking God for mercy for them when they are going through their processing and let them break! Let them crumble! Let them fall down and skin their knees! That is how they will learn to overcome adversities.

It is how they will appreciate what their leader/mentor has been through and appreciate the sacrifice. It is how they will be matured to represent the Kingdom and their King well! Recognize that when you are the leader or mentor for such an individual, you need to:

1. Stop entrusting them with any further responsibility – if you continue to do that, all you are doing is setting yourself up for an even bigger betrayal and let down and everything you teach from that point will be used against you and the vision God has given you.

2. Stop trying to coax them into understanding your position or point of view. Remember Matthew 7: 6.

When they have gotten to the point where they do not appreciate the value of the training they are receiving, they will not appreciate anything else. That is the time you must relinquish any false hope you have of trying to change them for them to see your point of view. <u>*You cannot fix a person, nor can you save them, that is God's job!*</u> You are not qualified or capable of changing a person – that is the job of the Holy Spirit. Your role is to sow the seed, not try to make the plant grow. Remember 1 Corinthians 3: 5 – 7.

Address the individual and speak to them about

    a. What is expected of them,

    b. What they need to do to improve and

    c. The importance of following the instructions given to them and

    d. The need for them to follow through and finish the process.

Once you have done that, then the onus is now on them to make a decisive effort to accept correction and make a change. It is also now in God's hands completely to deal with them should they continue along the wrong path. That is designed to take the stress from you and allow you to focus on those who appreciate your attention, the value of your training and time.

Know this:

1. You are not a hypocrite nor an evil, mean wicked person when you leave someone for the Lord to deal with.

2. You need to stop praying for God to show mercy and start praying for him to increase the fire, to keep the process going and ask Him to grant them the grace to go through it and still stand.

3. We also as leaders need to ask the Lord to help us to discern when to let go and when to hold on and fight. We need to ask Him to help us to understand or remember what real love is. Real love is not only about John 3: 16, it also includes 1 Corinthians 11: 32, Hebrews 12: 6, Revelation 3: 19 and 1 Corinthians 5: 1 - 5

The Word of God in the New King James Version (NKJV) speaks of the refining or of being refined altogether 19 times, and most often in reference to silver and gold. If we are to come out as PURE GOLD, we have to be willing to be refined.

The process of refining is necessary when something is crude or unfinished. Recognize that something has to be refined for it to be usable. For example, when oil is discovered/found, it is crude. That means that there is a mixture of fuels of different kinds all mixed together, which, on its own cannot be used; and the process of refining means that these different kinds of fuels must be separated, converted and treated so that it can meet the requirements of the user(s).

Crude oil cannot be used as is – it must be processed. It is a highly variable mixture of heavy and light hydrocarbons that need to be separated in a refinery to turn them into usable products. (Keyword: USABLE). As a result of all that, it is impossible to develop a universal boiler or engine capable of running on all crude oils.

S.O.A.R.

According to the Oxford Dictionary the word "soar" means "(to) fly at or mount to great height. (To) hover or sail in air without flapping of wings or using motor (engine) power."

According to the Merriam Webster Online Dictionary to *"soar"* means *"to rise or increase dramatically (as in position, value, or price); to ascend to a higher or more exalted level; to rise to majestic stature." (To) Increase rapidly above the usual level."*

In addition to that, Isaiah 40:31 says, *"But those who wait on the Lord Shall renew their strength; They shall mount up with wings like eagles, they shall run and not be weary, They shall walk and not faint."*

Eagles soar. We have the choice of walking at ground level with those who are too afraid to come out of their comfort zone and fulfill their potential, comfortable in their small corner of self, and unable to see the bigger picture of God's plan.

The Lord's will is that every Royal Daughter be willing to S.O.A.R. if she is going to fulfill her purpose as the daughter of the King of Kings. He wants every one of His Royal Daughters to accomplish their God-given purpose and walk in her calling, not just as a woman, but as a vessel of honor for the Most High God. He wants us to rise above the usual level rapidly; and the only way we can do that is to **S.O.A.R.**:

Submit   –   to God's Authority and the Kingship of Jesus Christ.

Obey   –   the Word, Instructions and Principles of the Lord (by reading His Word daily and staying in His Presence.)

And   –   (then after that)

Rise   –   above the obstacles, beyond your limitations

Deuteronomy 28: 1 – 14 reminds us of the blessings that are the result of a person's obedience to God.

Break The Cycle

Every time God raised up a deliverer to lead the Children of Israel and that deliverer carries out their assignment, they remained on a good path. As soon as the assignment is finished, and that leader passed away, the Children of Israel went right back into sin. Every time they went back on to the path of sin, the Lord allowed the enemy to pull them into bondage again; and when they cried out from that genuine place of desperation, He then raised up a deliverer. (Read the Book of Judges and 2 Kings 17 – 25). The nations have delved so deeply into sin, while at the same time, many are crying out to God for help and change. God is preparing deliverers He can raise up to bring deliverance to the people; but it is not going to be one man. He is preparing His believers – the Church – to be the deliverer of the nations. He has been preparing the saints – the true and faithful ones who, through their trials and challenges learnt how to *"bend a bow of bronze"*. They stood faithful – followed His instructions despite their personal challenges, despite the personal and corporate attacks, they stood and learnt how to fight and how to engage in spiritual warfare. In so doing, they are being prepared to boldly engage the enemy, stand up to today's Goliath and face not just the accusers, but also those who do not care about the God we serve, those simply determined to eradicate Christians and Christianity.

There a Spiritual fight and a Physical one that we will inevitably engage in – meanwhile we must maintain our faith, walk as disciples and ensure that our hearts are in the right place regarding our enemies so we do not lose the race. (Matthew 5: 43 – 48). That takes the kind of skill, discipline, determination and purity of heart and mind that can only come through our obedience, devotion, and absolute submission to God.

Faith In God For Purpose

Are you a parent? If you are then you are functioning in some level of Faith. How is that possible? You have been given the opportunity to bring change, add something positive, help turn situations around and even change the course of people's lives from a path of destruction to a path of life. You have been given the opportunity even to change the eternal destination of people you see/meet every day, and even for those you do not know and will never meet. You have been given a gift from God – because all life comes from God – as well as the privilege of training, nurturing and raising another human being – also known as – your child, using everything you know and have been taught, to train them for a time to come about which you know nothing, and for a purpose that you are not fully privy to or may not even know or understand. When you think about it, of course you are going to need God to help and guide you. He is the One Who created you, your child AND the father of your child. He knows your purpose and that of your child/children. You do not know what tomorrow really holds, we can only speculate. God is the only One Who knows everything about everything – future included!

Sometimes, when a child comes through painful circumstances – rape, abusive relationship – whatever the situation may be, some persons view the child as a reminder of something painful and a resentment toward or hatred for the child develops on the part of the mother who gave birth to that child. Some of us may think how can a mother hate her child?

But we have to recognize and accept two (2) things.

1. It is God Who gives Life, not the person who hurt you. God is the Creator of Life. A child is a gift from God with inherent and undeniable purpose, and oftentimes, that child coming out of that painful situation turns out to be one of your greatest blessings to you. Nothing can manifest, come to life, come to birth, nothing can happen without God's permission and nothing is a surprise to

Him. If He allows a child to come forth from that painful situation, then He also knows the purpose He put in that gift; He knows why He allowed him/her to be born and that in all of that, there is the potential for change and your blessings to come through that child. Ultimately, a child, despite the circumstances through which he/she came into this world, has the potential to effect change, affect nations and change the game in our favor to the Glory of God.

2. God is the Creator of Life, and God has a purpose for each life, AND He allows nothing to happen by accident - we need to accept and believe that.

3. GOD IS THE ULTIMATE PLANNER! What God orchestrates is excellent. He is the Beginning and the End and so He KNOWS the beginning and the end of all life. As such, God has already mapped out a path and provision for everything He allows. So even for the child we did not expect, He already knew their beginning and end and He has already made the provision for this child in this earth. Our inability to see that, does not influence or affect the provision He has already made. Unless our decision to not have any more children is as a result of a life-threatening situation, when we make those decisions, (citing economics or just not having the will to bother with everything that comes with raising a child) we are not only being selfish, but we are robbing the world of a potential problem-solver/solution to a problem we are in fact facing, and we could be robbing nations of a game-changer! What if Ehud was not born? What if Deborah was not born? What if Elijah, Elisha, David, Solomon,

Abraham, Sarah, Ruth, Esther, Naomi, Dorcas, John, Matthew, Mark, Luke were not born? What if Todd Dulaney was not born? Then we would not be singing *"Victory Belongs To Jesus"*. What if Apostle Dr. Steve Lyston and Bishop Dr. Doris Hutchinson were not born – would there even be a Restoration World Outreach Ministries Incorporated? What if Fred Hammond, T. D. Jakes, Sir Winston Churchill, Walt Disney, The Winans Family, Christine D'Clario, Kathryn Kuhlman, Billy Graham, your doctor, your best friend, your spouse wasn't born? What if **you** were not born? Imagine how many people would not have had the experience or benefit of you in their lives? Can you imagine the greatness that lies within you, that you cannot yet see, but that God already knows is within you, and how much He wants to bring it to fruition/manifestation? The greatness God put within you is about to come forth – Get Ready to S.O.A.R. in it!

A Queen In The Making

Recognize that you are indeed an Esther! Oftentimes persons believe that when we speak of Esther, it is usually and only about marriage – it is so much more than that. Esther was a woman who went through a process of learning how to be who God wanted her to be for Him.

Esther's training process took time, and patience was a critical element. Esther was being trained and molded with the resources of the king, and as such, even before she became the

Queen she was meant to be, she was benefiting from the King! She was a gem that was hidden only to be revealed in time!

As you prayerfully wait, do not let your zeal and expectancy fade. Instead, know that as you avail yourself to the Lord, His Word and His instructions, surely you will become the Queen He created you to be!   You are simply a Queen in the making! Keep standing in and for the Lord!

CHAPTER 11

Personal Protocols

The moment you surrender your life to the service of God through Jesus Christ, you are an ambassador for Christ and for the Kingdom of God. Every ambassador must maintain certain protocols because they are representing their nation and region at the highest level, and they are protecting the reputation of their kingdom. Everything they engage in reflects on their nation, their nation's leaders and their people.

It is imperative that you recognize you represent everything and everyone to which you are or will be connected – God, the Kingdom of God, yourself, your family, your church, your company/job, everyone who has vouched for you, recommended you or stood as a guarantor for you. You represent your gender, your past schools and everything you will connect with in the future.

As *Royalty In Motion*, you must know how to operate in any given environment and be able to deal with persons, groups or situations at any level across the board – and do so with a great deal of diplomacy, decorum and discernment. Doing that does not make you any less connected to reality, it does not make you a hypocrite – it just enlarges your territory and opens more doors for you to go through to reach more people for the King.

At the end of the day, how we carry ourselves, how we approach and respond to people, situations, our environment and our challenges on a daily basis – especially in times of adversity – speaks volumes for or against us; and all of that is important to the King. What is said about us and all that we represent, is determined by our actions and choices.

How We Carry Ourselves As Royal Daughters

Within the first few seconds of meeting, people form opinions about you based on your appearance and behavior. The way you walk, the way you carry yourself, the way you look, your smile, grooming, and your attitude toward others, are all taken into consideration. Whether fortunately or unfortunately, *"man looks at the outward appearance..."* (1 Samuel 16: 7) and determine a lot about you based on their first impression of you. I, for one, am grateful that the Lord does not judge us based on first impressions, but instead he searches the heart. The King of Kings knows the hearts of His daughters.

A positive, dynamic image will give you more self-confidence and help others to have more confidence in you too! Image, however, is more than appearance. By projecting the right visual and behavioral style, you can achieve a positive and lasting impression that will promote success in all that you do. Your image touches everything in your life.

For example, the way you dress and present yourself physically, makes a big difference in the way you socialize and connect with those around you. It also speaks volumes about you and how you operate in other areas of your life. That being said, recognize that your image should therefore send a clear, consistent message about who you are, what you have to offer and where you want to go.

Do not leave your identity up to fate and chance. Know who you are and who you want to be so that the image you portray is real. Smiling and maintaining eye contact are not only great ways to meet someone new, but they contribute to a great first impression.

Good Manners Will Take You Through The World

Growing up, one phrase that was constantly repeated by my parents was, *"Good manners will take you through the world!"* Our parents constantly said that to us because they knew firsthand that it actually did, and they wanted us to understand that and live by it. What that statement means is that even without qualifications, academic achievements or formal training in a subject, once you had good manners – once you were respectful, honorable in your actions and had good manners – that would open doors of opportunity for you anywhere. You could approach someone – a potential boss or persons having different levels of authority – and not have the academic qualifications required and because of the way in which you do what you do or approach them or resolve a matter for them, they willingly take you on to represent them or their organization as an employee.

Oftentimes people think that asserting themselves in an aggressive manner will show everyone around them that they can manage, or that they are in control; but all it shows is that they have a high level of insecurity and that they are afraid someone will find out they *cannot* manage. In addition to that, there are those who will try to manipulate others (particularly psychologically and emotionally) to do what they want them to do or to satisfy their own personal, ulterior motives. Manipulation is *not* a management artform. Instead, it is an unfair abuse of authority and influence over another person's free will and personal rights, or over a situation in an effort to achieve selfish gain – to make self "look good" at the expense of another person's character and freedoms. True royalty *does not* manipulate.

Maintain Honor

Honor is a principle that is very important to God our King, it runs throughout His Word. At least 39 books of the Bible mention the word "*honor*" in some way/form. God as our Father instructs us in Exodus 20: 12, *"Honor your father and your mother, that your days may be long upon the land which the Lord your God is giving you."* 1 Peter 2: 17 also says, *"Honor all people. Love the brotherhood. Fear God. Honor the king."*

Honor can lengthen your life and open doors – even bring you into the presence of great men. It was Joseph's honor for God that helped him to make the right decision to honor his master by rejecting the sexual advances of his master's wife. (Genesis 39: 7 – 10). Furthermore, although it didn't feel like it at the time, he made the right choice, and the end game was his ultimate victory. The honor code he lived by caused him to rise to become Prime Minister in a foreign nation – second only to Pharaoh, and elevated above his previous master. That shows us that regardless of the immediate personal cost, we must maintain honor for God, and He will vindicate us in due season and elevate us.

Honor

One of the things that sets us apart and identifies us as true Christians and as Godly leaders is our understanding and application of the principle of honor to our lives. Everything we do and say, MUST express HONOR; Honor to God, honor for our leaders, and must show self-respect and respect for those around you and those to whom you are connected.

When you Honor, it is the Word of God in Action! Your service speaks volumes for you.

Every commandment given, every instruction of the Lord, every principle of God is about honoring the Almighty and Most High God.

Learn How To Honor God First

When we learn how to honor God then we will not want to do anything to hurt or disappoint Him - we would do anything to please Him. We want to ensure that in representing the Most High and Most Excellent God that we are above reproach, living as He instructs so that we do not misrepresent Him and bring reproach to His Bride – the Church/the Body of Christ.

Honoring God *includes*:

1. Studying and Abiding by His Word – applying the principles of His Word to our daily lives honors Him.

2. Honoring others as His Word requires

3. Gathering in the House of God

4. Respecting God's Servants

5. Being diligent in executing His instructions

6. Being faithful to Him

7. Fasting

8. Praying

9. Obeying and Respecting those set over us

1 Timothy 6: 13 – 16 says,

"I urge you in the sight of God who gives life to all things, and before Christ Jesus who witnessed the good confession before Pontius Pilate, that you keep this commandment without spot, blameless until our Lord Jesus Christ's appearing, which He will manifest in His own time, He who is the blessed and

only Potentate, the King of kings and Lord of lords, who alone has immortality, dwelling in unapproachable light, whom no man has seen or can see, to whom be honor and everlasting power. Amen."

(Just a note that *"Potentate"* means *"sovereign ruler"*)

When we honor God with and in every area of our lives, He releases His blessings to us and fulfills His promises to us. In addition to that, others will recognize His excellent greatness and the manifestation of that in our lives and seek to know and serve Him.

Honor Your Father And Mother

Exodus 20: 12 says, *""Honor your father and your mother, that your days may be long upon the land which the Lord your God is giving you."* (See also Ephesians 6: 2)

This scripture speaks not only of the physical, but also of the spiritual parents as well. Hebrews 13: 17 clearly states, *"Obey those who rule over you, and be submissive, for they watch out for your souls, as those who must give account. Let them do so with joy and not with grief, for that would be unprofitable for you."*

Royalty understands the value of following the instructions of their parents because God assigned their parents, so that they would have the DNA He needs them to have and the right lineage to allow them to fulfill their purpose and His will.

Honor And Respect Your Elders

1 Timothy 5: 17 says, *"Let the elders who rule well be counted worthy of double honor, especially those who labor in the word and doctrine."*

One of the first social things we are taught is how to honor our elders. As children we are taught how to speak to adults with respect and with the right tone: No sarcasm, no shouting at an adult or talking down to them; No walking away when an adult is speaking to you – things like that which show respect brings honor and glory to God ultimately. But even more than that the Word speaks about the elders being those who operate in the House of God and the Body of Christ.

We must recognize that every relationship we have is training for our relationship with God; and also, that those set over us at any given point could not be there without God's permission. His Word in Romans 8: 28 reminds us, *"And we know that all things work together for good to those who love God, to those who are the called according to His purpose."* That being said, in every situation/challenge we face, the question for us becomes, *"What am I to learn from this situation Lord?"*

Honor Your Masters

1 Timothy 6: 1 says, *"Let as many bondservants as are under the yoke count their own masters worthy of all honor, so that the name of God and His doctrine may not be blasphemed."*

Your boss, your supervisor, the leader of your nation; God allowed him/her to be in that position for a reason. Remember that what you mete out to others, that is what may be meted out to you when you come into a position of leadership. In other words, what goes around comes around.

We may or may not like those set over us, but the Lord may allow you to be under their charge because He wants you to learn something from them and learn how to work with those you may not agree with or like. Understand that Leadership is not about having only the personalities you like around you. It is about working with those around you to get the mission accomplished despite personalities and opinions.

Honor True Widows

1 Timothy 5: 3 reminds us to *"Honor really widows."* Give them respect and care for them. Ensure they are cared for every opportunity you get.

Simple Manners And Basic Etiquette

Without hesitation I will be the first to tell you that I am not the authority on Manners and Etiquette, but there are a few things I have been taught (by others and by the Holy Spirit) that have worked well for me and I would like to share them with you.

Remember, good manners can take you very far and open doors of access for you that no glowing recommendations

from others can do. We may not always get it right, but always be willing to try.

Familiarity breeds contempt. Be respectful when addressing others in any position of authority – whether publicly or privately, and use their titles unless they tell you otherwise. Furthermore, never assume that because you are familiar with the personal life and circumstances/details of someone, that it gives you the right to drop their titles, talk down to them, or speak to them as if you are all on the same level. Until otherwise indicated by them, you are not "pals", so you address them accordingly. *Dr. So-and-So, Ambassador So-and-So, Apostle So-and-So*, and in circumstances where there are no official titles or you do not know a person's title, until they tell you otherwise, you address them using basic titles such as Mr., Mrs., Miss, Brother, Sister – depending on the environment.

Personal Protocols For Life

When you are staying at someone else's house:

Remember that they have developed their own system of operations in their home environment, they know why they do what they do. Where you feel that you can make things more efficient for them by making some changes – with all your best intentions – do not simply jump in and begin to make those changes. You could be doing more harm than good for them. Ask them how they want it done, or if it is okay for you to do whatever it is you are thinking. Be ready and willing to accept their NO and respect their decision. It is their right.

Do not "bark orders" at your host, or dictate what they should or should not do in their own place of abode – even if they are family, or are younger than you. Maintain respect at all times. Furthermore, respect other people's property. Regardless of how close you are to someone, you must treat whatever they lend to you or allow you to have or use with respect – take good care of it. For someone else, they look at how you treat what they have lent or given to you as a reflection of how you value the relationship you have with them. If you have children, even if your children are free to run amuck at home and do whatever their hearts tell them to do, recognize that not everybody does things the way you do, so when in their zone respect that. Teach your children how to be cognizant of respect the rules of others or the wishes of others.

How We Speak To Others

We are in a culture today where the goal is to get to a certain level of familiarity with those around you and build a good team and grounds for better communications. In an effort to do this, oftentimes lines are crossed and lines of demarcation that ensure respect is maintained are blurred. As a result, everyone – children and adult - see each other as being on the same level.

Speak to others with respect. When you are responding to someone senior to you, whether in age or authority and when you are not familiar with the person you are speaking to, ensure you remember to say,

- ✓ Yes Sir, No Sir

- ✓ Yes Ma'am, No Ma'am
- ✓ Yes Mr. Senior
- ✓ No Mrs. Elderly
- ✓ I Don't Know Sir
- ✓ Ok, please give me a moment to check for you Ma'am.

These responses seem to have become obsolete in communication in society today. Sadly, there are many factors that contribute to this breakdown, but we must never lose our commitment to honor and respect, particularly in how we address each other.

According to Exodus 20: 12, 1 Timothy 5: 1 and Titus 2: 2,

- ✓ It is not okay to hit or curse a senior (Remember also Proverbs 20: 29)
- ✓ It is not okay to hit, curse or dishonor your parents in any way. (Remember also Genesis 9: 22 – 24)
- ✓ It is not okay to be disrespectful to those set over you
- ✓ It is not okay for you to rebel and bring others with you into the rebellion

CHAPTER 12

Are You Royalty In Motion?

The Heart of *Royalty In Motion*

The heart of a Royal Daughter – the heart of *Royalty In Motion* - must be pure before the Lord. Her heart must be one with the heart of her King; so she genuinely loves what He loves and hates what He hates. (Remember Psalm 119: 104 says, *"Through Your precepts I get understanding; therefore I hate every false way."*)

<u>The heart of Royalty In Motion goes after the King</u>, she pursues Him with great passion and zeal because her heart trusts her king. She knows Him in the secret place and looks forward to go into the secret place.

<u>The heart of Royalty In Motion is yielded to her King</u> without hesitation or fear because she knows that whatever He does is well done, and whatever He is doing for her or with her, she can rest

assured that she is well taken care of – positioned and covered by her King and Creator.

The heart of Royalty In Motion is wise – like the heart of Abigail. According to 1 Samuel 25, Abigail was able to diffuse a potentially violent situation after her husband, Nabal, publicly disrespected and rejected a servant of the Lord. She knew the consequences of such actions, so she brought a peace offering (of sorts) to David and his men and took care of their immediate needs. She stepped up where her husband fell short. Sadly, her husband was unrepentant and filled with pride, and as a result his lack of humility, he was struck by God and died. Abigail exercised great wisdom in how she approached David to dispel the matter and protect her family from David's wrath and ultimately the hand of God moving against her household.

There are some Royal Daughters that have been oppressed and held back by the Nabals in their lives. But notice that despite Nabal's actions and attitude, Abigail employed great wisdom in how she dealt with him. As you stand in your Spiritual position with grace and obey the instructions of the Lord, He will show you how to deal with such challenges in your marriage and household and cause you to have great victory.

Royalty In Motion also need to have pure, repenting, clean, and forgiving hearts. Without a pure heart, you will not be able to see purity beyond the mess you encounter every day! And it is hidden in there somewhere – we are prime examples of that. Without the repenting heart, we have hardened hearts and there is no room for love or forgiveness in a hardened heart. Without a clean heart, we make the wrong choice, engage in the wrong activities and our minds, emotions and spirits become corrupt! (Psalm 51). Without the forgiving heart, we simply cannot forgive and will be unable to move from where we are spiritually, emotionally and even physically in our lives and remain in the past while growing bitter. We have to recognize that if we do not forgive, we cannot be forgiven.

<u>*Royalty In Motion must receive healing – emotionally, mentally, and spiritually!*</u> Hurting people hurt people, and what we have been through or are going through - instead of becoming bitter and unforgiving about it ~~all~~ - we must be willing to forgive, love and move on and instead seek to use those experiences to bring healing to others instead of increasing and perpetuating hurt! Oftentimes the internal pain and suffering we endure through a broken heart or two, deception and so on, influences our decisions in other areas and that can be dangerous if there are deep hurts and pain. The Lord wants to do some healing today.

<u>*Royalty In Motion needs to be transformed by the renewing of her mind!*</u> If we are not willing to renew our minds, we will constantly be holding on to the past and our view of everything we encounter will be tainted/skewed. We will be faced with hopelessness; there will be a constant fight with rejection, anger and will become unteachable and cease to learn and grow! We will be conforming to the world instead of being transformed through the constant change of mindset! Conformity stunts/hinders our growth in any area!

How we view things determine the outcome of (and how we handle) the various situations we face daily.

Royalty In Motion needs to be thankful/grateful/appreciative. God did not have to give us the gift of Life, but He did, and He added purpose to it. He did not nave to allow us an opportunity for salvation, but He did and because of His gift, we can walk in victory over sin. He did not have to bring us out of the situations we found ourselves in but He did. If we did not have a process to go through; if we did not have the challenges we have faced; if we were not held under for one reason or another, then you would not have grown the way you did, you would not have a testimony with which to encourage someone else, you could not be promoted. Everything you have gone through has served to mature you. Be grateful for all that God has done in you and for you.

Royalty In Motion Is A True Worshipper

A true worshipper does not wait on a song to pump them up into a frenzy so they feel good enough to give God worship. God deserves to be honored with our worship, not because of how we feel, but because we know He deserves to be worshipped and glorified. When we begin to recognize that God, the All-Powerful, Majestic, Invincible, Infallible, King of Kings, Who reigns over the entire universe, chose to take the time and fearfully and wonderfully make us, and that He loves each of us beyond measure and has plans to bring out the greatness He put into us, then we will begin to appreciate Him. When we begin to appreciate Him, and the mercy, grace, strength and favor He has extended to us, and the gifts He has given us, and the benefits that He loads us with every day, then we will desire to worship Him with every step we take, every moment we breathe. A true worshipper does not wait for service on Sunday for a "worship session." A true worshipper worships God in everything they do with everything they have and they are not afraid or ashamed to be and do just that.

Realize that True Worship has nothing to do with the songs we sing, how up-to-date the song list is and how well they are sung and all the riffs and runs that can be done in them. True worship is not about how well we play the instruments – in fact, true worship has nothing to do with a song. True worship has everything to do with the state of our hearts. (*Psalm 15; Psalm 24: 3 – 6*), and the heart of *Royalty In Motion* is for her Creator and King and always desires to please Him and worship Him.

Anybody can shout a praise while they are in malice with someone; but true worship exposes the heart and its contents and commands total honesty before God as we enter into His Presence. We are required to go before Him with the right heart, the right spirit, the right attitude and with humility, recognizing that without the Almighty God our Creator, we are nothing (*Isaiah 6: 1 – 5*). David reminds us in Psalm 51 that it is when we have a new and clean heart that and yield to our Creator and King that our joy will be restored and we will be able to teach others the right way and bring souls to Him. (*Psalm 51: 10 – 13*)

Worship is a lifestyle. We live worship, not have worship. Everything about us must worship God, our lives, our attitudes, our relationship with God, our relationship with others, fasting, prayer, reading the Word are all part of Worshipping God. When we take the time to enter into the Presence of God, we must be willing to be honest with Him and pour out our all for

Him – we must be willing to share with Him our deepest love and admiration for Who He is to Him without fear or pride. We should never be embarrassed to tell Him how we feel about Him and how much we appreciate Him and His love, grace and mercy for us. We must also be willing to spend time there with Him.

The King of Kings is also the Lord of Lords. God is King, and God is Spirit – and so He must be worshipped in Spirit and in truth. So, there is a spiritual aspect involved in serving the King. We cannot separate the natural part of our lives from the spiritual part.

Royalty In Motion is a true worshipper and knows that worship is a vital part of maintaining a strong relationship with God her King. She highly values worshipping God. She knows it's a lifestyle. Therefore, *Royalty In Motion*:

Honors God in and with every area of her life. She knows that God requires holiness (*1 Peter 2: 9*), and so, she knows that her lifestyle must be holy according to God's standards. As part of a "royal priesthood" Royalty In Motion has to lead by example. She reveres God and respects His Word, His work, His people, His house, His Apostles, Prophets and servants everywhere at every level. She lives holy and does not engage in adultery or fornication. She gives God her best at all times. She ensures that the quality of what she is giving to God is always the best and she seeks always to function in excellence to the glory of God her Father.

Walks in Obedience to God and His Principles and Instructions. Obedience to God is a most important aspect of worship.

Is a Giver. Royalty In Motion is not afraid to give because she knows where her help comes from. David was a true worshipper and he gave all and gave the best when he was giving unto God. In 2 Chronicles 23: 14 – 16 says, *"David was then in the stronghold, and the garrison of the Philistines was then in Bethlehem. And David said with longing, "Oh, that someone would give me a drink of the water from the well of Bethlehem, which is by the gate!" So the three mighty men broke through the camp of the Philistines, drew water from the well of Bethlehem that was by the gate, and took it and brought it to David. Nevertheless he would not drink it, but poured it out to the Lord."* Royalty In Motion understands that everything she has belongs to God (*Exodus 9: 29; Psalm 24: 1 – 2; 1 Corinthians 10: 25 – 28*) and that He is the Source of everything, and gives us the power to get wealth. (*Deuteronomy 8: 18*). She also understands that God not only extends Grace and Mercy to us, but His Divine Favor as well. (*Genesis 23: 1 – 12; 2 Chronicles 1: 1 – 12; Psalm 5: 12; Psalm 30: 5 – 7*).

Royalty Knows Where To Draw The Line

Royalty in Motion embraces her value and does not allow anyone to compromise that. She understands that according to the Word of God in Psalm 139: 13 – 14, she is fearfully and wonderfully made, and embraces God – Father, Son and Holy Spirit – without apology, as her Creator and the Sustainer of her life, the Author and Finisher of her faith, as her Strength. Her

King is the First Love of her life, as her Father and her King. She embraces the fact that her body is a precious gift from God and does not lower herself to the common level of allowing every man that she knows to put his hands on her body, let alone sleep with her. Instead, she guards and protects this priceless treasure – her body – for the king God is preparing to find her and value her has she ought to be valued, and honor her for the rare gem that she has been become while serving diligently in the Presence and in the House of God.

Royalty In Motion does not give in to her emotions and spill all her business over social media when she is angry. She is confidential so she does not use social media to air her dirty laundry or vent about all the things negatively affecting her, or tell every detail of what is going on in her family – that is what Prayer is for, and praying must be one of her biggest weapons.

Know this: Where the Word of God says in Proverbs 18: 22, *"He who finds a wife finds a good thing, and obtains favor from the Lord."* Understand, that should never be offensive to any woman, especially women today. You are not being treated as an object, you are being treated as someone of value. The thing that is referred to that he will find is not you but in finding you, he will find a good thing called a relationship – a union. We all know that whenever something is just handed to us we take it for granted easily, sometimes even without knowing it. When you have to work for/toward something, when you have to fight for something or seek after something, you place greater value on it because you know what it took to acquire or accomplish it.

Royalty In Motion

1 Corinthians 11: 7-9 says, *"For a man indeed ought not to cover his head, since he is the image and glory of God; but woman is the glory of man. For man is not from woman, but woman from man. Nor was man created for the woman, but woman for the man."*

Royalty In Motion does not allow just anyone to put hands in her hair, on her feet or in her hands, or body for that matter. Instead she discerns and she asks the Lord to direct her on where to go, with whom to go and what He wants her to do.

The Character of Royalty In Motion

Royalty In Motion knows she has many imperfections and is not afraid to acknowledge or admit that. She knows that she does not know it all but knows and accepts the One Who does - the only Wise, Almighty, Omniscient and Omnipresent God. As such, she knows the importance of maintaining a strong relationship with God and always chooses to seek and honor Him first. She knows that what God says is truth and never fails, so she stands on Matthew 6: 33, Psalm 115: 3, Psalm 121 and Romans and is constantly abiding by Psalm 23 and Psalm 51.

Royalty In Motion leads by example – good example. She controls her tongue and does not engage in gossip/talebearing. She ensures that her speech is always with grace (Colossians 4: 6).

Royalty In Motion bears and functions according to the Fruit of the Spirit. (Galatians 5: 16 – 26). She walks according to the Word of God and allows herself to be molded by Him through the application of His word to her life. Obedience is her key!

Royalty In Motion

Royalty In Motion knows that she has the potential to function and make decisions based on her emotions quite readily, so she relies on the instructions of the Holy Spirit of God to teach, direct and guide her in her actions and responses.

Royalty In Motion knows that her worth is not determined by the opinions of others but by what God, Her Creator and King says about her. (*Psalm 139: 13 – 15; Proverbs 31: 10 – 31*)

Royalty In Motion does not allow her environment and circumstances to limit her or determine her worth. She knows and accepts that Her Father – Her King – is limitless. She knows that according to Genesis 1: 28, it is within her DNA to go beyond limits set by anyone, including herself. She knows that she can do all things through Jesus Christ Who strengthens her. She knows that as she stays *In His*

Presence, she can call upon her Father and King at any time to enlarge her borders and territories, increase in her and increase her, to cause her to go beyond expectation and achieve greatness, all for *His* honor and glory – and not hers.

Royalty In Motion recognizes that she is a vessel of honor that must be yielded to her Heavenly King, and submitted to her earthly authorities. She knows that being submitted to the leadership of her Shepherd/Apostle/Mentor and the headship of her husband does not diminish her value and demean her capabilities, but protects her virtue and matures her to fulfill her purpose. She allows God to choose for her so that she can walk in His will for her.

Royalty In Motion

Royalty In Motion is constantly moving with the flow of God, always seeking to follow the instructions of God; She constantly pursues the Presence of God, the Will of God, the Timing of God and is always seeking to fulfill the purpose of God on her life. She is the queen who is not afraid to get in the trenches with others and does what it takes to accomplish what God has instructed. She is not hesitant to do what God says and is willing to go with her king – her husband – wherever God takes them for God's will can be accomplished through them both as a unit.

Royalty In Motion, fights for her family, and treats her family like the God-given gift it is. As such, she teaches her sons and daughters – biological, foster or adopted – how to be the kings and queens God has created them to put Him first in all areas of life. She teaches them how to honor, respect and obey God in every area of life with everything God has given them. She teaches her children to know their worth and protect it. She stands with her husband unafraid to submit to him according to the Word of God, and knows how to speak life over him despite what she sees.

Royalty In Motion is an Intercessor and a Spiritual Warrior who knows the value and power of prayer and the fact that Prayer to Almighty God works! She is a fighter who trusts God *"to teach her hands to make war that she can bend a bow of bronze"* so that she can protect what God entrusts to her.

Royalty In Motion recognizes that she will make mistakes from time to time but also knows that learning from her mistakes and moving forward despite her shortcomings will cause her to finish the race well.

Royalty In Motion does not compete with her king and her royal brothers but complements her king – working with him rather than against him, praying for him when he cannot find the words to speak about or does not want to share what hurts, disappoints or discourages him. She encourages her king in times of adversity rather than release negative words or curses at him. She operates in Godly wisdom in dealing with the king God has placed in her life as husband and honors her husband in word, thought and action. She prays for her kingly brothers always knows how far to go with them – protecting her honor and shunning the very appearance of evil. She recognizes that she is one of the doors that guards her family and makes every effort to keep the enemy out and her family secure.

Royalty In Motion stands with her royal sisters and loves them, not look for every opportunity to tear them down. She is not threatened by them or their gifts, talents or potential, because she stands confident in her difference and the knowledge of who God has created her to be. She does not fight against her royal sisters, she prays for them and speaks God's will over them, because she recognizes that they too – like her – were created for a purpose. She knows when to embrace her sisters and how far to go with them. She knows that she cannot divulge every bit of information to and knows that they too were created for a purpose. She is not afraid to tell them the truth with Godly wisdom.

Royalty In Motion

Royalty In Motion, knows that she has the potential to be attacked and used by the Spirit of Jezebel (*1 Kings 16 – 21, 2 Kings 9 and Revelation 2: 20*), so she makes every effort to stay in the Presence of God, (*Acts 3: 19*) and allow Him to work on her heart, process her and refresh her with His Word and through the experiences He allows her to go through. She knows that all things work together for good to them that love the Lord. (*Romans 8: 28*)

Royalty In Motion has the God-given, God-ordained capacity to be a daughter, sister, wife, and mother, and she also recognizes that our limitless and loving God has equipped her to be much more than can be imagined. She can function in many different roles all at the same time – businesswoman/entrepreneur, strategist, logistics expert, teacher/educator, therapist, homework expert, chef, political leader, social worker, facilitator and a catalyst for change to help the poor and needy, empower others, promote justice for the voiceless, faceless, homeless, widowed, orphaned and oppressed – all while she maintains her queenly status in the sight and Presence of God.

Royalty In Motion knows that a queen remains a queen in the Presence of the King.

You have tremendous potential and capacity for greatness yet to be revealed. The authority you carry is not light by any measure. As His Royal Daughter you represent the King of Kings. Go! Be! Do, what God says!   Exude the grace, poise, strength, sophistication, character, wisdom and inner beauty of God's Royal Daughter.

Whether you do so by fact or by faith, declare it with your life and with your lips, "I AM ROYALTY IN MOTION!"

Bibliography

Hayford, Jack W. Executive Editor, *New Spirit-Filled Life® Bible*, (New King James Version) © 2002 Thomas Nelson, Inc.

Pfeiffer, Charles F., Vos, Howard F., Rea, John. Editors, *Wycliffe Bible Dictionary*, (Seventh Printing) © 2005 Hendrickson Publishers, Inc

Price, Paula A. (PhD). *The Prophet's Dictionary: The Ultimate Guide To Supernatural Wisdom*, © 1999, 2002, 2006 Whittaker House

Slater, Sharon. *Stand For The Family*, (Fifth Edition) © 2010, 2016 Inglestone Publishing

Concise Oxford English Dictionary, Eleventh Edition. © 1964, 1976, 1982, 1990, 1995, 1999, 2001, 2004 Oxford University Press. All Rights Reserved.

https://www.biblestudytools.com/dictionary/marriage/

https://www.dictionary.com/browse/motion

https://www.scienceabc.com/humans/baby-grow-womb-9-months.html

https://en.wikipedia.org/wiki/Jochebed

https://en.wikipedia.org/wiki/Biblical_judges

Royalty In Motion

www.ingramcontent.com/pod-product-compliance
Lightning Source LLC
Chambersburg PA
CBHW051838090426
42736CB00011B/1866